For Agro &
Big Chris

The Kingdom That Was,

And Is,

And Is To Come

Alexander M. Billups M. Ed.

Dedication

To King and Country

CONTENTS

Part II: THE KINGDOM THAT IS

Part III: THE KINGDOM THAT IS TO COME

Preface

I stand on the shoulders of great men. Men who have come before me in the study of the Kingdom of God. Scholars such as the late Dr. Myles Munroe of Bahamas Faith Ministries, David Pawson a world renowned British theologian, Bishop N.T. Wright a spirit-filled Bible scholar who served as the Anglican Bishop of Durham, Dr. Michael Brown a doctor of Hebrew and Semitic languages and many others have helped me discover the most important theme in the Bible. Through their audio, video and literary works I have come to understand that throughout history many Christians have made the mistake of creating religious doctrines that are slightly askew of the Bible's main focal point. Although many denominational founders have meant well the effects have been nothing short of division and confusion within the body of Christ.

I have authored this text in an attempt to shed light on the Kingdom of God concept found within the scriptures. This concept runs through both the Old and New testaments like a golden thread that binds the two together. Christ the Messianic King, is certainly a dominant theme in both testaments of the Bible but we have often failed to grasp what exactly He is King of. Jesus is God the Father's appointed King sent to represent Heaven on Earth. He completed His priestly work during His first advent and He will set up His visible Kingdom at His second coming. We know this, but one simple truth that most people miss is that although Jesus did not assume the throne 2000 years ago it doesn't mean that He is not the King over all; He is.

This book was created in an effort to help earnest men and women see just that.

It is my prayer that you would take this work as an offering of love and friendship. I am not a world class scholar like the aforementioned men so please take any mistakes I have made with a grain of salt. I enjoy the word of God but I am learning more everyday as I suppose you are as well. Throughout reading this text you may notice that I try to use capital letters when referencing the Lord in anyway; bear with me. This is something I do simply to reverence His sacredness.

Thank you for taking the time and I am sure you will find this book well worth your study.

Your brother,

Alexander Billups

Introduction

What is the Kingdom of God concept?

God's righteous government over every facet of the entire earth by the power of His Holy Spirit through the administration of His Son King Jesus and the redeemed royal family; with the intention of making the visible earth an exact replica of the invisible country of Heaven to the praise of His glory forever.

That's a long sentence. I know. Here is the short version:

God ruling by the Spirit from Heaven, Jesus ruling on earth, the saints ruling with Jesus, in order to make the world like Heaven.

Use either definition you like but the point is the same; God is setting up His Kingdom on Earth. He has been doing this work since the dawn of creation and everything will culminate with the mission accomplished. The Kingdom of God is the main theme of the entire Bible. It is so important that it was Jesus Christ's one and only public message. Upon my inspection of the King James Bible, the interchangeable terms of Kingdom of God and Kingdom of Heaven were mentioned: 50 times in the gospel of Matthew, 15 times in the gospel of Mark, 39 times in the gospel of Luke and 5 times in the gospel of John. This count does not even include the times Jesus was referred to as a King or the "Son of David."

The establishment of the Kingdom of God on earth is the reason why God made humanity in the first place. It is the reason why men were endowed with the earth. It explains the reason for the nation of Israel's existence. It is the reason Jesus came and atoned for our sins. It is the reason the Holy Spirit was poured out on the day of Pentecost. It is even the reason we have the Bible. At last, it is also the reason Jesus will come one final time.

A Christian may think this is common information but I encourage the reader to think again. How much of our church doctrine is focused on escaping the fires of Hell and spending an eternity in Heaven? If Jesus only spoke of The Kingdom of Heaven then why does our preaching and evangelism major on topics other than the Kingdom? How often is it clearly explained and made practical in our Bible studies? How many courses do our current seminary institutions have on it? The truth is we often major on the minors and forget what is major. By losing sight of the Kingdom of God leaders in Christendom have developed independent and often conflicting explanations of many biblical teachings. The Kingdom of God concept serves as the proper framework through which we are to understand the entire text of scripture. Moreover, It operates as a practical lens through which the believer can view and impact his or her world.

Let us now being a brief yet exciting journey through the Bible to see how the Kingdom of God begins and how it will all finally end. This book is not for the faint of heart or dull of mind so grab your Bible and a coffee. Be prepared to be challenged, stretched and changed.

Part I

The Kingdom that Was...

Chapter 1

The Earth is the Lord's!

(Sketch for Peace Descends to Earth 1852)
Ferdinand-Victor-Eugène Delacroix

The gospel that we have been preaching and teaching for a very long time is incomplete. As a result, the outcomes that it has produced, while quite remarkable, have been stifled. In order to get to the bottom of this we need to simply begin with the end in mind.

First and foremost, the correct title of the gospel is actually **the gospel of the Kingdom of God.** The term *"Gospel"* simply means good news; but the question is good news about what? Good news about salvation? Good news about healing? Good news about grace? The answer is all of these and much more.

The message that Christian disciples are to proclaim is this; **Jesus Christ is the King of the earth right now**. Not later, now. Take a minute and allow that to soak in. Just imagine if everyone across the world got the news tomorrow morning that Jesus, of the Bible, is in fact King of the entire earth. How would the world look different? What would be different in society? How would governments be different? How would family relationships be different? How would financial transactions or commerce as a whole be different? Well, this is precisely the message that we are to preach. Jesus Christ of Nazareth, the son of David, is the King...TODAY! He rules over all of the earth, the produce derived from the earth and the people on the earth. King Jesus reigns, but the problem is most of the people in this world-system are unaware of this. They are still under an old regime.

The situation is illustrated in two scenarios that come to mind. First, take the incident where God stripped the Kingdom of Israel from King Saul. Due to his fear of people's opinion, God refused to allow him to govern the people any more. God sent the prophet

14

Samuel to give him this news but in spite of the message King Saul still wanted to keep up appearances. He requested Samuel walk with him in front of the people to give the impression that God was still with him when in fact God had already given the kingdom to another. The people saw Saul on the throne but God knew the truth. Saul's reign was over. David was the new anointed king even though he was an outcast. Saul had the look but David had the power. We will explore this illustration in further detail later, but for now, just hold the mental picture of the false king and the true king on the earth at the same time and you can easily understand how the people were misled.

The second illustration that captures the essence of this situation can be seen in the history of the United States of America. On September 22nd 1862, the first Emancipation Proclamation notice came as an executive order from the desk of President Abraham Lincoln. This ground breaking order immediately liberated all of the African American slaves in the southern states of America. It became the law of the land that black men and women were free. While the order went forth in 1862 the slaves in the south were not physically freed until well after 1865 when the 13th amendment abolished slavery. The owners in the southern states did all they could to maintain control over these people and keep them oblivious to the truth. The confederate generals were in direct rebellion against the American government which resulted in the outbreak of the Civil War.

These two events capture the essence of what has been happening on earth since King Jesus arrived on the scene. He Himself proclaimed, "All power and authority in Heaven and on Earth has been given unto

15

Me; therefore go into all the world and make disciples of all nations…" Such a bold statement is not relegated to a future time. It is in the present tense. In fact, it is the motivation behind evangelism. The disciples were armed with the knowledge of the good news about the Kingdom. **Jesus declared that God the Father had given Him all authority. Therefore, He personally authorized His followers to go out into His territory and teach the occupants about the King.**

The Apostle Paul clearly understood this mission when he stated to the Roman church,

> *"Through Jesus, the descendent from the royal line of King David, we have received grace and our office of apostleship* **to call all the nations to obedience to this way of life.** *This brings glory to the name His name."* (Rom. 1:2-6 NIV)

Before we go any further, it is critical that the reader understand a subtle but major distinction in terms in order to avoid confusion. **In the Orthodox Jewish Bible the terms for "world" and "earth" mean two different things.** The word for earth is "Haaretz" and it means *the land* or the physical terrain. The word for world, on the other hand, is "Hazeh" and it indicates **the world-system** or the current systems that govern the resources of the earth. (Munroe)

Take note of the difference:

> *"In the beginning Elohim (God) created hashomayim (the heavens, Himel) and* **haaretz** *(the earth)."* (Gen. 1:1 OJB)

As opposed to,

16

*"Do not have ahavah (love) for the Olam **Hazeh** (this current world-system), neither the things in the Olam **Hazeh**. If anyone has ahavah for the Olam **Hazeh**, the Ahavas [Elohim] HaAv is not in him."* (1 John 2:15 OJB)

I point out this distinction because as you the reader will soon discover, while the earth is the Lord's the battle for which world-system that will govern its resources rages on. It is in the world-systems of darkness that Satan claims his victims and creates mischief.

One final question that I would like to pose in laying the groundwork for this text is; **why** did God the Father create the Earth in the first place? What was His motivation? This question must be at the forefront of our minds because it is the rationale behind all things. After careful study I believe I have found the answer to this most pressing question. **God the Father made all things as a gift to the Son He loves**. Not just the Earth either, but all of creation was created as a gift for Jesus Christ.

In a letter that Paul wrote to the Colossians he states the following,

*"For by Him (Jesus) were all things created, that are in heaven, and that are in earth, visible and invisible, whether they be thrones, or dominions, or principalities, or powers: all things were created by Him, **and for Him**. He is before all things and by Him all things are held together."* (Col.1:16-17 NIV)

God the Father sanctioned the creation of all things as an offering to His beloved Son. What an extravagant gift!

Now that we understand God's motivation behind creation we can pinpoint who these possessions were intended for. All things belonged to Jesus Christ. **God the Father knew that in due time Christ would come through the lineage of men and rightfully claim the inheritance that was prepared for Him from the very beginning.**

Chapter 2

Oh Adam, Where art Thou?

(The Creation of Adam on the Sistine Chapel ceiling 1511)
Michelangelo Buonarroti

God's Kingdom plan began with Adam. Adam was not just another creation but he was the crowning jewel of creation. The whole universe served as a ring housing in which Adam was placed as the finishing touch of God's brilliance. He bore God's image as the masterpiece of creation. His body was a temple perfectly fit for God Himself to dwell in; and that was exactly the idea. At the appointed time, Christ the eternal Son would step into creation, take up residence in a body and claim His inheritance forever. Adam was no ordinary creature; he was God's son.

"Kenan was the son of Enosh. Enosh was the son of Seth. Seth was the son of Adam. **Adam was the son of God.** *"* (Luke 3:38 NIV)

He was not the "Son of God" in the sense that Christ is. Christ is co-eternal and co-existent with the Father in the office of the eternal Word (Memra). Adam on the other hand was God's son in the sense that God made Him without earthly parents and placed in him the spark of life which begets life. Nonetheless, this fact does not detract from Adam's uniqueness at all. The man was something special.

Adam's home was Eden. It was the place he was fitted for and it was where he was always meant to be. **Eden means Paradise.** It was an abundant place filled with all of the resources and pleasures anyone could want. Fresh clear water, ripe fruit, aromatic trees, healthy animals, blue skies, and a moist parcel of earth all given to a young man whose body would never wear out. In Eden there was no crime, no pollution, no death, nor diseases of any kind because man had committed no sin. It was a place of green abundant life not decay and death. Most importantly, God's presence was there, and God loved Adam. He loved him so much that God made

20

him on the sixth day of creation and stopped everything
to rest with him on the seventh. That means that Adam's
first full day of existence was a Sabbath day of rest in
which he and God walked together in fellowship all day
long. Eden was what you would call a little piece of
"heaven on earth."

After the day of rest God put Adam to the test. It
was time for Him to show Adam what he was equipped
to do. God put so much untapped potential in Adam it is
mind boggling. The Lord gave him the task of naming
the animals and this brought out the potential hidden
within. (Munroe) Without any formal training he could
function just like the God who created him. He could
comprehend, identify, synthesize data, sort, classify and
communicate his rational. God trusted the potential
within Adam so whatever he called the animals that is
what God agreed they would be. Such a feat of
intelligence was only the beginning of Adam's abilities.

God's lists of responsibilities for Adam were to,
"work the garden, till the ground *(Haaretz)*, protect it,
fill the earth, dominate over it, be fruitful, and multiply."
God gave him **legal authority over all of the earth.** To
put it another way; Adam was a king!

Read the following:

"The highest heavens belong to the LORD, but
the earth He has given to mankind. *" (Ps. 115:16 NIV)*

"...What is mankind that You are mindful of
them, human beings that You care for them? You have
*made them a little lower than angels and **crowned them***
with glory and honor. You made them rulers over the
works of Your hands; You put everything under their
feet*: all flocks and herd and the animals of the wild, the*

21

birds in the sky, and the fish in the sea, all that swim the paths of the seas." (Ps. 8:4-8 NIV)

*"Then God said, "Let Us make mankind in Our image, in Our likeness, **so that they may rule** over the fish in the sea and the birds in the sky, over the livestock and all the wild animals, and over all the creatures that move along the ground." So God created mankind in His own image, in the image of God He created them; male and female He created them. God blessed them and said to them, "Be fruitful and increase in number; fill the earth and **subdue** it. **Rule** over the fish in the sea and the birds in the sky and over every living creature that moves on the ground."* (Gen 1: 26-28 NIV)

Adam a was king indeed. Before the reader assumes I might be misapplying the title of "king" let's simply define exactly what that term means. A king is: a sovereign male ruler who has inherited his position by birth right. It is usually held that God Almighty has established his throne (seat of vested power). He is charged with the task of dispensing righteous judgement throughout his sphere of authority. He is the head of a "kingdom" where he provides resources, protection and guidance to his subjects and or family members. He is not just the manager of the resources under his care but he is actually the owner. The subjects of the kingdom are to honor him for his care, thank him for his resources, emulate his customs and honor his God. Adam was guardian of the earth and a ruler just like his Father. He was a king.

Adam's task was to make the entire earth look just like Eden. God did not tell Adam how to do this He simply gave him the commands, resources and mental capacity to do the work. What a wonderful opportunity this was for Adam to use his endowments to spread the Paradise of God. Adam did not need a laundry list of laws to govern him because God breathed His Spirit into him. He was enlightened. He intuitively knew what to do. The infinite gifts of "mind", "will" and "emotions" were all inside of him. All he had to do was stay connected to the presence of God and all would be well. This was the life that flowed from God to Adam continually. It was the source of his brilliance, power, youth and innocence. As long as Adam stayed obedient to God the Father the presence of the Spirit stayed within him.

Bad news, Adam failed. Once he committed an act of disobedience sin entered into the human race. The punishment that God levied on all sin was death. This consequence was not because God is vindictive but because God is life and to disobey life is to disconnect from life. Instead of Adam being a living man on planet Earth he became a walking dead man, a ghost in a shell who was cast out from the presence of God. He was no longer the ruling king that God gave dominion to but rather a shadow of his former self. He became an, angry, insecure, accusatory, cowardice sinner who was enslaved to his desires.

I know these are hard words but re-read Genesis chapter 3 and the truth of these adjectives becomes evident. The king of the earth had been bested by a cunning adversary and according to the enlightened apostle, "...whomever you yield yourself to as a servant, to him you become a slave once you chose to obey him."(Rom 6:16) Jesus also confirmed this in stating, "Whoever commits sin becomes a slave to sin." (John 8:34) So **Adam was no longer in charge of himself let alone the territory he was meant to manage. He had**

23

forfeited his inheritance to the one who defeated him; Satan.

I am sure the reader might have some questions at this point. Questions such as, "Who is Satan? Where did he come from? Why did he trick Adam? Why was he against Adam and God? Why did God allow this?" and so on. All great questions indeed. I will cover these as we progress but for now just remember the old adage: "to the victor goes the spoil."

In summary, **God made the world for Christ. He then gave it to Adam in anticipation of Christ's arrival. Adam lost control of the earth to Satan and it became Christ's primary goal to get it back.**

Chapter 3

The Devils Made Me Do It

(Illustration for John Milton's Paradise Lost 1866)
Gustave Dore

Satan has always tried to overthrow God's Kingdom. He has opposed its establishment at every stage throughout history. Here is a statement from Genesis about how the kingdom of darkness ruled right before the flood:

"Now the whole earth was corrupt and filled with violence..." (Gen. 6:11 KJV)

Sounds pretty bad right? It was. Humanity is currently moving more and more in this direction every day, but believe it or not things were much worse back then than they are now. In fact, Jesus stated that before His return to earth the human condition will once again resemble those treacherous *"days of Noah."* During Noah's time period men were wild and wicked. The thoughts of their minds were only continuous streams of evil. People built civilizations, probed all kinds of curious arts, mastered metalworking, engaged in great music and revelry but all for the purpose of selfish glory. The gift of brilliance that God gave to mankind was never rescinded because His gifts are without repentance. However, He did feel sorrowful that He made humanity because everyone seemed to use their brilliance to advance wickedness and promote bloodshed on the earth. **This was not God's plan but men enslaved to sin create world-systems that promote evil.**

It was not just the unrestrained passions of inflamed men that hastened the downward spiral mention in Genesis chapter 6 but there were more menacing foes at work. **Demons were a major driving force to the chaos that covered the earth.** It is written that the "Sons of God saw that the daughters of humans were beautiful, and they married any of them they chose…" (Gen. 6:2) Certain angelic host called the "Sons

26

Daughters of Man = Cain's line
Sons of God = Adam's Line.

of God" apparently had access to the earth and they are to be blamed for much of the madness that ensued. The book of Job validates that angels are referred to as the "Sons of God" and that Satan was once numbered among them. Jesus even spoke of angelic abilities and said that He witnessed Satan "fall from Heaven like lightning." It was a group of these fallen angels who looked upon women, desired them and made the choice to procreate with them. How this was done remains a great mystery but two suggestions can be put forth and either one may be plausible.

First, **they could have had the ability to change form**. Often in the scriptures angels take on the appearance of normal men. Consider the following: three "men" appear to Abraham, Jacob wrestled with a "man" all night, two "men" appeared to Lot prior to the destruction of Sodom, and a "man" with a sword in his hand appeared to Joshua before a battle. Furthermore, the writer of the letter to the Hebrews went so far as to say that we must treat strangers well because sometimes we unwittingly entertained angels. Lastly, Paul's teachings suggest this is the case. He taught that Satan himself has the ability to "transform" into an angel of light and it has been postulated that he admonished women to cover their glorious hair so they won't tempt the angels who are watching over them.

Secondly, **the fallen angels or "Sons of God" could have possessed normal men**. While the concept of angels possessing humans is not explicitly found in scripture, it need not be completely ruled out. Angels are spirits and spirits can and do occupy the bodies of men. Consider the spirits of the men themselves, unclean spirits, demonic spirits, the Holy Spirit, and Satan (a fallen angel) entering into Judas at Christ's betrayal.

(John 13:27)

27

Either way, it was a commonly held belief among the Apostles, the early Church and ancient Jewish sages that this bizarre event did in fact occur.

Jude states in his letter to the believers:

*"I want to remind you that after The Lord had delivered His people out of the land of Egypt, He destroyed those who did not believe. And **the angels who did not stay within their own domain, but abandoned their proper dwelling**, He keeps under darkness, in eternal chains for judgment on that great day. **In like manner**, Sodom and Gomorrah and the cities around them, who indulged in sexual immorality and pursued strange flesh, are on display as an example of those who sustain the punishment of eternal fire. ..."* (Jude 1:6-7 NIV)

In context, the apostle is warning about sexual sin. He cites the Israelites who died due to their sexual sin and Sodom and Gomorrah who suffered punishment for sexual sin as well. It then stands to reason that the phrase "...in a like manner, they left their first estate or did not stay within their own domain" implies that the fallen angels casted off something in order to indulge in darkness. In doing so, they became enslaved by the passion they yielded to. This suggests that the words **"chains of darkness"** convey a rather riveting truth. Such powerful chains can bind any man or angel who chooses to fulfil their own inordinate desires.

An early Church Father Justin Martyr wrote in his letter to the Roman Senate:

*"But the angels transgressed this appointment, and **were captivated by love of women, and begot children who are those that are called demons**; and besides, they afterwards subdued the human race to*

28

themselves, partly by magical writings, and partly by fears and the punishments they occasioned, and partly by teaching them to offer sacrifices, and incense, and libations, of which things they stood in need after **they were enslaved by lustful passions***; and among men they sowed murders, wars, adulteries, intemperate deeds, and all wickedness. Whence also the poets and mythologists, not knowing that it was the angels and those demons who had been begotten by them that did these things to men, and women, and cities, and nations, which they related, ascribed them to god himself, and to those who were accounted to be his very offspring, and to the offspring of those who were called his brothers, Neptune and Pluto, and to the children again of these their offspring. For whatever name each of the angels had given to himself and his children, by that name they called them."* (The Second Apology of Justin Martyr)

Considering the fact that this letter was written around 150 A.D. by a man who died for his faith, it is wise to give it the credence it deserves. **Justin was very close to the time of the Apostles and he offers us a peek into the prevailing theology of the day.** According to the Martyr the offspring of the women and the fallen angels were called "demons." Therefore, the term demon is not interchangeable with the title of angel. This makes perfect sense considering the fact that the word demon is variant of the Greek word *daemon* which spoke of demigods in classical Greek thought. These demigods were half gods and half men who allegedly inhabited the earth. They were the force behind extremely powerful men and fanciful tales that have captured the imagination for millennia. It seems that the doctrines of the demons always have a way of resurfacing in various forms. Even today, they continue to seduce the hearts of men away from the King of kings.

The text of the Jewish Midrash contains some interesting statements regarding this phenomenon as well:

"Then two angels, Shemhazai and Azazel, came before G-d and said, "Did we not warn You before You created man, saying, 'What is man, that You should be mindful of him?'" G-d replied: "Then what shall become of the world?" "We will suffice instead," they replied. G-d answered, **"I know that would you live on that world, the evil inclination would rule you just as much as it controls man, but you would be even worse."** *But the angels persisted, saying: "Let us descend to the world of men, and we will show You how we will sanctify your name." And G-d said: "Go down and dwell among them."* **Sure enough, as soon as the angels descended, their evil inclination overpowered them.** *When they saw the beautiful "daughters of man,"* **they became corrupted and sinned with them. They and their descendants are the Nephilim"**

(Midrash of Shemhazai and Azazel)

The interpretation of this text as the others is hotly debated but when all three are viewed in light of each other a rather compelling case can be made. The concept of angels cohabiting with women was a matter of fact to many Christians and Jews. That said, I too take it as the most reasonable and concrete explanation for the existence of demons as well as the power and knowledge they possess.

In the Bible, the demonic souls that were produced by women and angels inhabited giant physical bodies that grew out of control. They were known as a race of Nephilim or Gibborim. The term Nephilim means "earth born or fallen ones" and the Gibborim is the offspring from angels and people. **The Nephilim were giants and they were the people who inhabited the ancient lands.** They had many clan names such as the Anakites in the Bible and they wreaked havoc throughout the world. All over the globe archaeologist have uncovered massive structures and skeletons which suggest that life on planet earth was once very different from we call normal today. Humans still do not possess the knowledge or machinery needed to build some of the monolithic edifices that have been found. In addition, each indigenous culture produced by this world-system has "folklore" tales of floods, giants and god-men walking the earth. Many of the deities that people worship right now are the spirits of the departed god-men who founded their cultures! Very curious, indeed.

Final thought on this subject for the moment, it is interesting to note that David became famous because he slayed Goliath. The reader should recall here that Goliath too was a giant. He and his four brothers were sons of Gath.

The scripture states of him:

"A champion named Goliath, who was from Gath, came out of the Philistine camp. His height was six cubits and a span. He had a bronze helmet on his head and wore a coat of scale armor of bronze weighing five thousand shekels; on his legs he wore bronze greaves, and a bronze javelin was slung on his back. His spear shaft was like a weaver's rod, and its iron point weighed six hundred shekels. His shield bearer went ahead of him." (1 Sam. 17: 4-8 NIV)

This man was huge. He was well over 9 feet tall and he had six fingers on each hand. In keeping with the

Kingdom of God, consider this: David was launched into renown by defeating the Philistine giant. The giants were the bodily descendants of the Nephilim who were inhabited by demons. **King Jesus, the Son of King David's bloodline, also gained fame by exercising authority over those same demons spirits**.

After God sent the Great Deluge on the earth He began to repopulate it with human beings descending from the family of Noah. Interestingly, we find that in the newly filled world giants still existed. They were not as large as in the pre-flood days but they still existed. This could be explained in a very simple way. If the genetic material of humanity had been tainted already then it is quite possible that these traits still existed in one of the wives of Noah's sons. Through selective breeding, recessed genes could easily become more dominant. Every herdsman knows this truth and I am sure that the demons did as well. Not to mention that although the flesh of the giants was destroyed in the flood the demonic spirits that inhabited the Nephilim were still alive. As the waters abated they were actively looking for new bodies to possess.

It is often said that the truth is stranger than fiction and in this case that statement just might be right.

Chapter 4

A Covenant with Abraham and Who?

(The Sacrifice of Isaac 18th Century)
Christian Wilhelm Ernst Dietrich

33

After Adam, God moved the focus of His Kingdom establishment to Abraham. The Lord had to use a man because it was the legal condition that He Himself put in place. Remember, *"The highest heavens belong to God but the earth He has given to man."* God's words are a law even to Himself. (Munroe)

This was not a problem seeing that the Father had His eyes on the perfect candidate. About 400 years after Noah God chose another man named Abram who was also "righteous" in his generation. He was not perfect but he was striving to do right in a world gone wrong. God graciously befriended this man and made him a promise in exchange for the man's trust and obedience. Abram accepted the terms and it was counted as "righteousness" in the sight of God.

The convent was simple:

*"Now the Lord had said unto Abram, Get thee out of thy country, and from thy kindred, and from thy father's house, unto a land that I will shew thee: And **I will make of thee a great nation**, and **I will bless thee**, and **make thy name great**; and **thou shalt be a blessing: And I will bless them that bless thee, and curse him that curseth thee: and in thee shall all families of the earth be blessed**."* (Gen. 12:1-3 KJV)

God appeared to Abram again and gave him more details concerning the covenant which were recorded in Genesis chapter 17:

*"When Abram was ninety years old and nine, the Lord appeared to Abram, and said unto him, I am the Almighty God; walk before Me, and be thou perfect. And I will make My covenant between Me and thee, and will **multiply thee exceedingly**. And Abram fell on his*

*face: and God talked with him, saying, as for Me, behold, My covenant is with thee, and thou shalt be **a father of many nations**. Neither shall thy name any more be called Abram, but **thy name shall be Abraham**; for a father of many nations have I made thee. And **I will make thee exceeding fruitful**, and **I will make nations of thee**, and **kings shall come out of thee**. And **I will establish my covenant between me and thee and thy seed after thee** in their generations for an everlasting covenant, to be a God unto thee, and to thy seed after thee. And I will give unto thee, and to thy seed after thee, the **land wherein thou art a stranger, all the land of Canaan**, for an everlasting possession; and **I will be their God**." (Gen 17:1-8 KJV)*

If we examine the terms of the contract closer we can see the following provisions promised in exchange for obedience:

- *Land*
- *His descendants would be a great nation*
- *Personal and familial blessing*
- *A great name*
- *He would be a blessing to others*
- *God would support him by blessing or cursing those who did likewise to him.*
- *In Abraham all of the families on earth would be blessed*
- *He would have numerous children*
- *Abram took the name Abraham by faith because he would father many nations*
- *He would be the father of kings*
- *God would be his personal God and he would be God's chosen*

35

- *The land where he was a stranger would become his*
- *The territory of Canaan itself would become his*
- *His seed would defeat all of his enemies and his children would inherit their land*
- *The covenant would be established with him personally and his "Seed" after him*

The Lord gave Abraham such great and precious promises. Since the quality of the gift reflects the heart of the giver, this act of generosity tells a lot about the type of person God is. Abraham began to experience the fulfilment of the promises through God's miraculous provision but things really got interesting when Isaac, the promised child, was born. **It was through Isaac that the royal line would be established and eventually the promised "Seed" be born.**

We are given a clear picture about who this future Seed is referring to in the drama of Abraham offering his "only son" as a sacrifice on the altar to the Lord. God stopped Abraham from completing with his hands what he had already done in his heart. However, where Abraham's knife was stopped God's wrath would go on to finish the job. God would one day sacrifice His only Son Jesus Christ for all men. **Just as Isaac was the "promised son" through whom the promised Seed would enter the world so Christ was the promised Seed through whom all of the promises of Abraham were destined to find their fulfilment.**

*"Scripture foresaw that God would justify the Nations by faith, and announced **the gospel** in advance to Abraham: "All nations will be blessed through you." So those who rely on faith are blessed along with Abraham, the man of faith... Christ redeemed us in*

*order that the blessing given to Abraham might come to the nations through Christ Jesus, **so that by faith we might receive the promise of the Spirit**...The promises were spoken to Abraham and to his Seed. Scripture does not say "and to seeds," meaning many people, but "**and to your Seed**," meaning one person, who is Christ."*

(Gal. 3:16 NIV)

Very few people have ever known the laws and promises of God better than the academically trained Pharisee Saul of Tarsus. He made the connection that most Jews have missed until this day; **Jesus Christ was the promised "Seed" that God the Father was referring to when He swore to bless Abraham.** The totality of the Abrahamic covenant was not directed only at one person but actually two people. That said, all of the promises made to Abraham directly apply to Christ the Seed as well. It would therefore be scripturally accurate to read the Abrahamic Covenant in a way that appropriated the promises to Jesus Christ.

Now read the following:

- *King Jesus would inherit land (Ps. 2:7-8)*
- *His descendants would be a great nation (Rev.1:6)*
- *He would receive personal and familial blessings (John 15:23-24)*
- *He would have a great name (Phil.2:9-11)*
- *He would be a blessing to others (John 8:12)*
- *God would bless or curse those who did likewise to Him (John 3:18)*
- *In Jesus all of the families on earth would be blessed (Isa. 49:6)*
- *Jesus would have numerous children (Matt. 18:3)*
- *King Jesus would father many nations (Isa.9:6-7)*
- *He would be the father of kings (I Pet. 2:9)*

- *God would be His personal God and He would be God's chosen* (Luke 9:35)
- *Land where He was a stranger would become His* (Ps.18:43)
- *The territory of Canaan itself would become His* (Matt. 5:35)
- *His seed would defeat all of their enemies and His children would inherit their land* (Mark 16:17 & Matt. 5:5)
- *God the Father would establish this covenant with King Jesus personally and His seed after Him.* (Gal. 3:16)

Something that is even more magnificent about the passage in Galatians chapter 3 is that it gives us a fuller and more robust picture of the gospel message. It states that the promised Seed, who is Christ, would bring the Spirit of God back to mankind. Paul associated the outpouring of the Holy Spirit with the fulfilment of the Abrahamic Covenant. The same Spirit that empowered Adam before he fell into sin was going to be restored to humanity. **God restoring the Holy Spirit to man was a precursor to an even greater miracle; the restoration of all things back to Adam's pre-fall conditions.**

Right about now, I anticipate that the reader may be doing a lot of thinking and that's a good thing. However, the most important question that a scholar should have is this, "does the Bible actually say these things; can they all be proven?" I have provided references so you can verify the claims that I have asserted thus far. I encourage you, the reader, to diligently search the scriptures at this time to see if those things I am saying are so.

Chapter 5

A Church in the Wild

(The Gathering of Manna 1896-1902)
James Jacques Joseph Tissot

God is faithful to His Word. Just as He promised, **Abraham's descents grew to be a large nation and the Kingdom plan was well under way.** The nation came to be known as the children of Israel because they all came from the common patriarchs Abraham, Isaac and Jacob (whose name God changed to Israel). It was from this nation that God the Father would establish the royal family line of the coming "Seed" to whom the promises of Abraham were entitled. It was through this family all that Adam lost would be restored.

The nation of Israel's population grew to about 3 million people while they were in captivity in Egypt. When God called them out of slavery they left with a significant amount of treasure from the Egyptian people. Imagine the sight, a bunch of slaves leaving the country with jewels and gold and no place to go! They were delivered by God's miraculous power and walking towards a "Promised Land." They had no list of directions; they simply had to follow a cloud by day and a pillar of fire by night. They never knew exactly when the cloud would move or the direction in which it would travel. But, once it did, all 3 million of them had to stop whatever they were doing, pick up camp and follow. Despite the obvious liabilities of such a journey, everything began rather smoothly.

According to the Bible, **the nation of Israel was actually the first "church." They were "called out" of Egypt as the assembly of God.** The word church finds its roots in the Latin word ekklesia meaning "called out ones." This fact is a shock to many people but study the following statement Stephen the Martyr made when he was interrogated:

"This Moses whom they refused, saying, who made thee a ruler and a judge? the same did God send

40

*to be a ruler and a deliverer by the hand of the angel which appeared to him in the bush. He brought them out, after that He had shewed wonders and signs in the land of Egypt, and in the Red sea, and in the wilderness forty years. This is that Moses, which said unto the children of Israel, A prophet shall the Lord your God raise up unto you of your brethren, like unto me; Him shall ye hear. This is He, that was in **the church in the wilderness** with the angel which spake to him in the Mount Sinai, and with our fathers: who received the lively oracles to give unto us..."* (Acts 7:35-38 NIV)

Paul the Apostle supports this notion and even goes on to explain to the Corinthian believers in detail how this happened:

*"For I do not want you to be ignorant of the fact, brothers and sisters, that our ancestors were all under the cloud and that they all passed through the sea. **They were all baptized** into Moses in the cloud and in the sea. They all **ate the same spiritual food and drank the same spiritual drink**; for they drank from the spiritual rock that accompanied them, and **that rock was Christ**. Nevertheless, God was not pleased with most of them; their bodies were scattered in the wilderness."*
(1 Cor. 10:1-5 NIV)

According to Paul, the people were "called out" of Egypt, baptized, and even took communion from an archetype of Christ. When the people drank from the living water which flowed from the rock it marked a spiritual transformation. Now, they not only shared in ethnicity but in a common spiritual identity and destiny. **They were destined to become the people of the Kingdom of God.** Through the baptism and communion the many individual people came to be viewed as one singular man in the sight of God. It is written: "out of Egypt have I called My son…" (Hos. 11:1)

The singular man concept explains why one man's sin could bring the nation down (Achan), one man's zeal could restore the nation (Phineas) and one man's worship could grant the people military victory (Moses). **The nation was one.** This idea is seen in other contexts until this day. These unified groups are referred to as "bodies". Think of a body of congress, a body of students, or a body of believers. All are one.

The truth about Israel being a church begs an additional question; **"If the nation of Israel was a church then is the universal church an Israel?"**

Paul seemed to think so.

*"Neither circumcision nor uncircumcision means anything; what counts is the new creation. Peace and mercy to all who follow this rule—to **the Israel of God.**"* (Gal. 6:15 NIV)

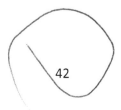

Chapter 6

Managing Jeshurun is No Fun!

(Victory O Lord 1871)
John Everett Millais

43

The Hebrew people were exactly like every other nation around them; pagan. **God the Father made it clear that He did not choose them because they deserved it but rather out of the kindness of His heart.** (Deut.7:7 NIV) What made them special was the God they came into covenant with. He Himself is special and thus everything He touches becomes blessed. After the Israelites came out into the desert plains they soon forgot about what God the Father had done and began to mumble against Him. The people had: a change in location, a change in destination, a change in occupation, a change in designation, and a change in material possessions but not a change in heart. They were the same old people but now they were covered in jewelry and Egyptian linen.

So what changed things? The giving of the Law. Moses, their leader at the time, was himself a type of Christ. He was summoned to a private meeting with God at the top of Mount Sinai which lasted 40 days. **At this meeting God showed Moses Heaven.** He showed Him what things looked like there and the hierarchical order of the celestial city. He taught Moses about the priesthood, praise, worship and sacrifice. God gave Moses universal laws of morality that spelled out what was bound up in the conscience of every human being: the difference between right and wrong, the knowledge of good and evil, the God honest truth. He even gave Moses national laws by which the people had to govern themselves in order to flourish. **God showed Moses the ultimate Kingdom IN Heaven**.

The Father says in reference to His glorious Kingdom:

*"**Heaven is My throne**, and the earth is My footstool. Could you build Me a temple as good as that? Could you build Me such a resting place?"* (Isa. 66:1 NLT)

As God revealed these glorious sights to Moses He also revealed the reason why He chose to invite him in the first place: **"See that you make everything after the pattern you saw on the mountain.."** (Ex. 25:40 NIV) This command of caution was repeated to Moses over and over. God was serious about the specifications of everything. He wanted Moses to **facilitate the building of the Kingdom of God on earth.** When Moses came down from the presence of God his face was shining with radiance. Earlier he received his calling but now he had a plan. Moses quickly and carefully began to put all of the pieces in place. The tabernacle, sacrifices, the Ark of the Covenant, the priesthood, the feasts and the Laws. God, in His faithfulness, was moving forward with His Kingdom plan and Moses was on board for the ride.

The people however were not so convinced:

"Why have you brought us up out of Egypt to die in the wilderness? There is no bread! There is no water! And we detest this miserable food!" (Num. 21:5 NIV)

Moses' position of vision bearer quickly disintegrated into a mere settler of disputes. The people complained because their hearts were not in the mission at all. They would rather have convenience, comfort and control. Even if it meant going back to Egypt which ironically offered none of these things. They were not interested in the journey of faith, they simply wanted to escape the taskmaster and get to the milk and honey. Things got so bad with this bunch that they reminisced about how "good" they had it in the Egyptian slave camps. Poor Moses! He had an uphill climb and it wasn't long before the stress of managing so many caused his own anger issues to surface.

Day after day Moses' face would glow from his meetings with God and by the evening the glory would fade under the flustering feuds of the Israeli family. His father-in-law saw that he sat all day as the primary arbiter for all 3 million people and recommended an alternative approach.

Here's the account:

*"The next day Moses took his seat to serve as judge for the people, and **they stood around him from morning till evening**. When his father-in-law saw all that Moses was doing for the people, he said, "What is this you are doing for the people? Why do you alone sit as judge, while all these people stand around you from morning till evening?" "Moses answered him, "Because the people come to me to seek God's will. **Whenever they have a dispute, it is brought to me**, and I decide between the parties and inform them of God's decrees and instructions." Moses' father-in-law replied, "What you are doing is not good. You and these people who come to you will only wear yourselves out. The work is too heavy for you; you cannot handle it alone. Listen now to me and I will give you some advice, and may God be with you. You must be the people's representative before God and bring their disputes to Him. Teach them His decrees and instructions, and show them the way they are to live and how they are to behave. But select capable men from all the people—men who fear God, trustworthy men who hate dishonest gain—and appoint them as officials over thousands, hundreds, fifties and tens. Have them serve as judges for the people at all*

*times, but have them bring every difficult case to you;
the simple cases they can decide themselves. That will
make your load lighter, because they will share it with
you. If you do this and God so commands, you will be
able to stand the strain, and all these people will go
home satisfied." (Ex.18:13-23 NIV)*

The advice that Jethro gave to Moses was good,
really good, but the truth is it was not God's best. We
see that Jethro was wise, efficient, an excellent manager,
and filled with sympathy but **the council he gave to
Moses was birthed out of human necessity not out of
God's ideology.** Moses had to set up a system of
government that dealt with the insolence and ignorance
of the people. **Judges are for people without
judgment.** Think of the implications of that statement. If
the people of Israel were all following the laws that God
gave Moses the positions of the judges would have been
completely unnecessary. Such is the case in our own
lives as well. The reason why we have supervisors on
the jobs where we work is because people cannot be
counted on to do their jobs by the book. The reason why
we have police officers is because people cannot be
counted on to follow the law on their own. **Thus, the
hierarchical system in which one human had to
govern over another was a clear indicator that
selfishness and ignorance still reigned within the
hearts of men.**

God allowed this accommodation for the same
reason that He allowed divorce to be permissible; due to
the hardness of the hearts of men. (Matt.19:8) This logic
goes so far as to explain the rationale behind the entire
book of Judges in the Bible. The prevailing philosophy
of the day was," there was no king in Israel and
**everyone did what was right in their own
eyes**…"(Judges 21:25 NIV) The citizens of the nation were

not law-abiding but rather a group of lost relativists with broken moral compasses.

Instead of a human serving as a divider of spoil and a settler of disputes God had a much better plan in mind. He told Israel through the prophets that the days were coming when no one would need to educate another person about God because every man would know about Him. The days were coming when the knowledge of God would cover the earth as the "waters cover the sea." The days were coming when God Himself would take out of man the stony hearts of rebellion and insert in men a new heart of flesh. **The days were coming when He would give men back the Spirit of God**.

Concerning the settling of trivial matters, Jesus too was bombarded with a similar situation. One day when He was teaching, a man wanted Him settle an inheritance matter between himself and his brother. Jesus quickly cut to the truth of the man's motivations. He proclaimed, "Man, who appointed Me as a judge or a divider of things between you two" and then He said to the crowd "beware of covetousness for a man's life does not consist of the abundance of the things that he possesses." (Luke 12: 14-15 NIV) **The King would not allow Himself to be distracted by the minutia of materialism. Instead, He brought out the truth that exposed the man's heart**. Jesus discerned that the man did not need a sword of justice to divide spoil but rather a sword of truth that would cut out his heart of greed.

To sum up, the judges that Jethro recommended and **the judges that God needed to raise up prior to the kings of Israel was a system of training wheels for people who were not ready to walk in God's Kingdom.** It was necessary because people who do not

48

listen to the conscience within need an external "voice of reason" to help them do what is right. The people had yet a long way to go before being Kingdom citizens but God's work with this nation was just beginning.

Chapter 7

Poor People Made Rich by the Kingdom of God

(The Ark Passes Over the Jordan 1896-1902)
James Jacques Joseph Tissot

The Father set Israel up to be the Kingdom of God on earth. They were positioned for success on a scale that this world had never seen. Not only did the people have a miraculous resurrection due to His "mighty hand and outstretched arm", they left Egypt with the riches of their oppressors. The miracles were a dazzling display of power and the wealth was wonderful but the most precious gift of all was what Moses was given on the mountain. **In the keeping of those Laws the people would find everything they would ever need.**

Etched in stone were these words:

1. *I am the Lord (King and Owner of all) you shall have no other gods before Me*

2. *You shall not make for yourselves any idol images to bow down and worship them*

3. *You shall not take the name of the Lord (King and Owner of all) in vain*

4. *Remember the Sabbath day to keep it holy; remember you were slaves in Egypt*

5. *Honor your father and mother so that things will go well and you will live long on the earth*

6. *You shall not commit murder*

7. *You shall not commit adultery*

8. *You shall not steal*

9.   You shall not give a false witness (lie) against your neighbor

10. You shall not covet anything that belongs to your neighbor

(Deut. 5: 6-21 NIV)

God gave the nation of Israel the Laws and blueprint to His Kingdom through the hand of Moses, the mediator of the contract. It is fitting to point out here that **the nation of Israel was not the Kingdom of God** but were the people group that God the Father selected to illustrate the government of His Kingdom to the world. The two are not the same thing. The covenant spelled out what Moses saw back on Mount Sinai. It was a pattern of the heavenly things he saw communicated in a way that human beings could understand. They were not the actual truths that Moses saw in the Kingdom **IN** Heaven itself but a shadow of the unseen reality.

In studying the fullness of scripture it becomes clear that Moses saw many things that appeared a lot like what John saw in the book of Revelations. Moses must have seen the High Priest presiding over a nation of priest. He saw God as King ruling over a royal family of kings. He surely saw a sacrificial lamb that was slain hence the sacrificial system of atonement. And no one would argue that he saw the most obvious of all, a glorious temple from which he drew the layout of the first tabernacle. **All of the things Moses made on earth were a shadow of the things he saw in Heaven but not the actual things themselves**. (Heb. 8:5 NIV)

Considering all of these blessings, being a national Jew had many benefits:

*"God committed to Israel **the adoption to sonship; the divine glory, the covenants, the receiving of the law, the temple worship** and **the promises**. Theirs are **the patriarchs**, and from them is traced the human ancestry of **the Messiah**, who is God over all, forever praised! Amen."* (Rom 3:1 and 9:4 NIV)

In this "Kingdom of God" archetype God the Father introduced a new world-system for the earth to be governed by. It was a heavenly order which entailed the following:

- *Moral Laws for conscience*
- *National laws for ethics*
- *Sacrificial laws for worship*
- *Dietary laws for health*
- *Sanitation laws for decency*
- *Military laws for safety and expansion*
- *Leaders for edification*
- *Business laws for commerce*
- *Relational laws for family well being*
- *Feasts for celebration and commemoration*
- *A Priesthood for intercession*
- *Prophets for direction*
- *A Temple as the center of all life in the Kingdom and above all this;*
- **God Himself reigned as King**

Upon close examination what we realize is that **God provided the layout for a government not a religion**. Although worship was commanded as a national practice this was done in reverence to the God-King *"YWHW ha Elohim"*. He alone reigned as King. The people were not to have a human king like the nations around them but they were to be different. Best of all, they were to teach the way of Kingdom of God to the nations around them. Israel was blessed to be a blessing.

Moses explained to them:

"See, I have taught you decrees and laws as the Lord my God commanded me, so that you may follow them in the land you are entering to take possession of it. **Observe them carefully, for this will show your wisdom and understanding to the nations**, *who will hear about all these decrees and say, "Surely this great nation is a wise and understanding people." What other nation is so great as to have their gods near them the way the Lord our God is near us whenever we pray to Him? And what other nation is so great as to have such righteous decrees and laws as this body of Laws I am setting before you today?"* (Deut. 4:5-8 NIV)

Because of the governing laws that were conferred on the people, Israel instantly had the opportunity to be the city set on the hill that would bring the light of God's Laws to the world. God set in front of the people the reward of blessings for obedience and the punishment of curses if they disobeyed. Moses hoped for the best but expected the worst. After years of administration and intersession he knew firsthand how "stiff-necked" this nation was. Before his death he prophesied:

"The Lord your God will raise up for you **a Prophet** *like me from among you, from your fellow Israelites. You must listen to Him. For this is what you asked of the Lord your God at Horeb on the day of the assembly when you said, "Let us not hear the voice of the Lord our God nor see this great fire anymore, or we will die." The Lord said to me: "What they say is good.*

54

I will raise up for them a Prophet like you from among their fellow Israelites, and I will put my words in His mouth. He will tell them everything I command Him."
(Deut. 18: 15-18 NIV)

We will see how well the nation of Israel exemplified the government of God's Kingdom to the other surrounding nations which remained trapped in this world-system. Let us hope for the best but I fear the reader already knows how this story will end.

Chapter 8

Purge Out the Giants!

(Joshua Ordering the Sun to Stand Still 1743-1744)
Joseph Marie Vien

After Moses' death **God moved the Kingdom mandate to Joshua.** He was Moses' servant and he was different that the other Israelites. He was a man of faith. God placed inside of him a "different spirit" than that of his fearful contemporaries. He believed that although Israel was a relatively small nation at that time God was with them and He would grant the people victory over any enemy they faced.

Joshua's job was that of a mighty warrior. He was selected to lead the people into the promised land of Canaan. There was only one very big problem. Giants were occupying the territory! Joshua had seen them with his own eyes because he was one of the men that Moses sent to scout the land about 40 years earlier. When the men came back they were terrified.

The Bible states:

*"They came back to Moses and Aaron and the whole Israelite community at Kadesh in the Desert of Paran. There they reported to them and to the whole assembly and showed them the fruit of the land. They gave Moses this account: "We went into the land to which you sent us, and it does flow with milk and honey! Here is its fruit. But the people who live there are powerful and **the cities are fortified and very large**. We even saw **descendants of Anak there**. The Amalekites live in the Negev; the Hittites, Jebusites and Amorites live in the hill country; and the Canaanites live near the sea and along the Jordan."*

*Then Caleb silenced the people before Moses and said, "We should go up and take possession of the land, for we can certainly do it." But the men who had gone up with him said, "**We can't attack those people; they are stronger than we are.**" And they spread among*

*the Israelites a bad report about the land they had
explored. They said, "The land we explored devours
those living in it.* **All the people we saw there are of
great size. We saw the Nephilim there (the descendants
of Anak come from the Nephilim).** *We seemed like*
grasshoppers *in our own eyes, and we looked the same
to them."*(Num. 13:26-33 NIV)

It was 40 years from that point and the fearful
older folks were now dead. A new generation of
Israelites were ready to march in by faith under Joshua's
command. This was the time to go in and possess the
land that God the Father promised to Abraham and his
children! God had personally cared for this estate
because **it was to be the future site for the Kingdom to
be established**. Just as He had prepared Eden for Adam
He had prepared the land of Canaan for the Israelites.
This would be the headquarters from which God would
influence the world through His people. But, first they
needed to clear out the giants.

Many people who read the Old Testament get
squeamish or sympathetic when they read these accounts
of conquest. They think, "How could a God of love
allow such violence?" Good question, but it shows that
the reader has not studied the context in which these
events took place. Remember our discussion of the
Nephilim back in chapter 3? These giants were the
descendants of the fallen angels and they were filled
with demons. **They committed all kinds of evil**
practices including burning their own children as
sacrifices to worship demonic entities. The idolatry of
the original people groups of the land knew no end.

In a warning God explained to Israel why He drove the Canaanites out of the land:

> **"Do not give any of your children to be sacrificed to Molek, for you must not profane the name of your God.** *I am the Lord.* *"'Do not have sexual relations with a man as one does with a woman; that is detestable. "Do not have sexual relations with an animal and defile yourself with it. A woman must not present herself to an animal to have sexual relations with it; that is a perversion. "'Do not defile yourselves in any of these ways, because* **this is how the nations that I am going to drive out before you became defiled. Even the land was defiled; so I punished it for its sin, and the land vomited out its inhabitants.** *" (Lev.18: 21-25 NIV)*

God had patiently waited for years in hopes that these people would turn from their wicked ways but to no avail. They were set in their ways and the blood they shed was defiling the good land that God nurtured. He set His face to judge them and then transplant in the land a group of people that would nurse it back to what He originally intended. This was the job of the Kingdom people who were coming in the name of the God of Israel. Ironically, this is the same calling of the Kingdom people of today. **We are tasked with going forth into Christ's land and reclaiming territory in order to bring it back under Divine control so it can flourish once more as God intended.**

Another fact that is interesting about Joshua is this: both Joshua and Jesus actually have the same name! In Hebrew the one name is Yeshua and it means "the salvation of God." The nation of Israel was God's son led by a warrior named "Jesus" and sent to dispense judgement on the wicked. The true Jesus Christ Himself went before them in order to guarantee an otherwise

59

impossible victory. In a christophany (Old Testament appearance of Christ) He even showed Himself in the form of a man prior to Joshua's invasion.

*"Now when Joshua was near Jericho, he looked up and saw **a Man standing in front of him with a drawn sword** in His hand. Joshua went up to Him and asked, "Are You for us or for our enemies?" "Neither," He replied, "but as **Commander of the army of the Lord** I have now come." Then Joshua fell facedown to the ground in reverence, and asked Him, "What message does my Lord have for His servant?" The Commander of the Lord's army replied, "Take off your sandals, for the place where you are standing is holy." (Jos. 5:13-15 NIV)*

Let me prevent any misconceptions by plainly stating that today God is not asking for the followers of Jesus Christ to engage in physical combat. This type of activity was clearly for a season and a reason. King Jesus told Peter to put up his sword and He taught the disciples to love their enemies. Vengeance belongs to Him alone and whatever is just Christ will execute upon His return. Nevertheless, the Christian believers are supposed to be warriors; just warriors of a different sort.

Chapter 9

Shattered Dreams

(The Bible Panorama 1891)
William A. Foster

God's Kingdom marched on. Through a series of marvellous victories Joshua did indeed take the people into the Promised Land.

Listen to the battle near Gilgal as one of the many examples:

"Joshua marched up from Gilgal with his entire army, including all the best fighting men. The LORD *said to Joshua, "Do not be afraid of them; I have given them into your hand. Not one of them will be able to withstand you." After an all-night march from Gilgal, Joshua took them by surprise.* **The LORD threw them into confusion** *before Israel, so Joshua and the Israelites defeated them completely at Gibeon. Israel pursued them along the road going up to Beth Horon and cut them down all the way to Azekah and Makkedah. As they fled before Israel on the road down from Beth Horon to Azekah,* **the LORD hurled large hailstones down on them**, *and more of them died from the hail than were killed by the swords of the Israelites."* (Jos.10:7-11 NIV)

There was no question that "The Lord Himself was fighting for Israel!" He commanded Joshua to be as exact in his warfare as Moses was in building the tabernacle. There were to be no peace treaties because if Israel failed to clear out these wicked nations God prophesied that intermarriage would soon take place. Unfortunately, **they did not obey**. The Israelites cleared **some** of the occupant nations but not all. It was instances of partial obedience such as this one that would prove to be the downfall of the nation.

As time went on, the Jewish people grew in number but struggled in solidarity. Many of them thought only of personal interest and neglected the Laws of Moses as well as the God who gave them. It was as if

God poured the new wine of the Kingdom into the old sinful wine skins of humanity and the bag was bursting at the seams. The people were not keeping the law, the priests were defiling themselves, the temple was desecrated, the judges were spurned, the people asked for human kings who turned to oppress them all while the weepy eyed prophets who warned of impending judgment were murdered.

Psalms 106 tells it best:

"They did not destroy the peoples as the LORD had commanded them, but they mingled with the nations and adopted their customs. They worshiped their idols, which became a snare to them. They sacrificed their sons and their daughters to false gods. They shed innocent blood, the blood of their sons and daughters, whom they sacrificed to the idols of Canaan, and the land was desecrated by their blood. They defiled themselves by what they did; by their deeds they prostituted themselves." (Ps.106: 34-39 NIV)

In all fairness, it must be mentioned that there were certainly many heartfelt and outstanding Jewish men and women in the Old Testament. Just consider people like: the Prophet Samuel, Queen Esther, the Prophet Daniel, King David and a host of others. God always had a group of people who loved Him and strove to serve Him no matter what. These faithful few often served as a witness against the masses who were degrading themselves by copying the evil customs of the heathen nations around them. Yet, it seemed that the more the few tried the worse the masses became.

The main problem that national Israel had was this; the hearts of the people were not changed. **They had all of the components of the Kingdom of God but**

63

not the Spirit of the Kingdom. Knowing this, God began to look to the future. He promised that one day He would make a new covenant with them. This agreement would be different from the old one because in the first one He had to treat the Jews as little children and "guide them by the hand" but in the new covenant He would not need to do this because He would give the people a loving heart and a desire to obey. (Jer. 31:31)

In addition, He promised that **He Himself would come to the people and help them finally become the people of the Kingdom of God**. He would do this through His Messiah. The "Arm of the Lord" would reach down and lift up His people to a height that their human frailty would never allow them to reach.

*"For to us a child is born, to us a Son is given, and **the government will be on His shoulders**. And He will be called Wonderful Counsellor, Mighty God, Everlasting Father, Prince of Peace. Of the greatness of His **government** and peace there will be no end. **He will reign on David's throne and over His Kingdom, establishing and upholding it with justice and righteousness from that time on and forever**. The zeal of the Lord Almighty will accomplish this."* (Isa. 9: 6-7 NIV)

God was coming to claim the throne. He would become King again. This promise became the national hope of the people. More than this, the coming King of Israel would also be the Ruler over the nations!

King David speaks in the second Psalm:

"I (God the Father) have installed My King on Zion, My holy mountain."

*"I (The Son) will proclaim the Lord's (God the Father's) decree: He said to Me, "You are My Son; today I have become your Father. Ask Me, and **I will make the nations Your inheritance, the ends of the earth Your possession**." (Ps.2:6-8 NIV)*

Under the Messiah's leadership Israel would become the epicentre of the world. The laws of God would go forth from Zion and the little Middle Eastern city on the hill would again change the world.

In reference to this Daniel foretold:

*"In the time of those kings, **the God of Heaven will set up a Kingdom that will never be destroyed**, nor will it be left to another people. **It will crush all those kingdoms and bring them to an end**, but it will itself endure forever." (Dan. 2:44 NIV)*

Chapter 10

All Hail; the King has Arrived!

(Jesus and NIcodemus 1898)
Henry Ossawa Tanner

After 400 years of silence **the King was finally coming**! The long awaited Messiah would deliver Israel from the hands of their Roman oppressors and bring them into a new era of power and glory the likes of which would put Caesar himself to shame! Or.... so the people thought. The King came in a way that was completely unexpected. As a normal person. He was born in a manger, grew up as a Torah observant Jew, and worked as a carpenter to make a living for His family.

This "King" was not much to look at. No glory clouds, no lightning, no noble steed, no trumpeters following Him around to announce the arrival of His royal highness...nothing. In fact, for the first 30 years of His short 33 year life span no one even knew who He was. What an odd way for God the Father to present His Son the King. Only one man had the inside scoop on Jesus and this man was making major waves in the Jewish community. He was considered a mighty prophet like Elijah of old and his words were just as coarse as the camel hair covering he wore.

His message was simple but powerful:

   "Repent! For the Kingdom of Heaven is at hand!!!" (Matt. 3:1-2 NIV)

John warned the people with tears in his eyes and passion in his heart that the King was coming. His Majesty was going to "thoroughly purge" all wickedness from Israel and **establish a Kingdom in righteousness.** There was no time to waste! John acted as a forerunner preparing the way. He cried, 'clean this place up, clean up your houses, fix up the roads so the King can ride in'.(Pawson) Most importantly, he commanded the people to clean up their lives. "Turn from your wicked ways and be baptized" he shouted. The coming of the King was certainly "good news" in Israel but the preparation for His arrival was serious business. John did not mince words. He told everyone that they needed to get things right with God. It didn't matter if they were soldiers or priests everyone needed to humble themselves in repentance.

After John baptized Jesus the forerunner's work faded into the background and the King took center stage. The King's baptism was different than all the others because it was at this special baptism that **the Holy Spirit from Heaven came down and rested on a man again.** The Spirit that enlightened Adam in Genesis was back. Moreover, the Spirit didn't just "rest" on Jesus but He was: filled with, driven by, spoke with and operated in the power of the Spirit. He was the only "living" man amidst the walking dead. His appearance may have been unbecoming but His words were different than anything the people had ever heard.

He opened His mouth and taught them saying...

"Blessed are the poor in spirit,
*for theirs is the **Kingdom of heaven**.*
Blessed are those who mourn,
for they will be comforted.
Blessed are the meek,
*for they will **inherit the earth**.*
Blessed are those who hunger and thirst for
righteousness,
for they will be filled.
Blessed are the merciful,
for they will be shown mercy.
Blessed are the pure in heart,
*for **they will see God**.*
Blessed are the peacemakers,
*for they will be called **children of God**.*

Blessed are those who are persecuted because of righteousness,
*for theirs is **the Kingdom of heaven**... "*

(Matt.5:3-10 NIV)

With statements like these and many others He taught the crowds about the Kingdom of God. Over and over He explained: what the Kingdom was like, how to get into it, who would be excluded from it and how **it would eventually be the only government left on earth**. Jesus certainly fulfilled this prophecy of Isaiah, "...unto us a child is born, unto us a Son is given and **the government shall be on His shoulders**..." The government of Heaven was all Jesus talked about. He spoke on this topic so much that Matthew makes mention of it 50 times in his gospel account alone! On one occasion when the disciples asked Jesus how to pray He responded,

When you pray say these words:

*"Our Father, who is in Heaven, hallowed be Your Name. **Your Kingdom come, Your will be done on Earth as it is in Heaven**... " (Luke 11:2-4)*

The Master knew exactly what His mission was and He made sure that the disciples knew that they had the same objective as He did.

What's more is that Jesus didn't just talk about the Kingdom of God but He demonstrated its power. With His words He healed the sick, raised the dead and performed many other miracles. When the people heard His teaching and saw the power that God the Father had given to Him "they were amazed because **He taught them as a person who had authority**..."(Matt. 7:28-29 NIV)

69

One of Jesus' most incredible feats was that He had the ability to cast out demons. The expulsion of these evil spirits was a great part of His work. Demons had been terrorizing people since the days of the Noah going from one victim to the next and now One greater than them had arrived. In the gospel texts we discover that demons were often (but not always) the main protagonists behind: **sickness, disease, violence, self-mutilation, addictions, seizure, blindness and even suicide.** While commoners looked upon these people as outcasts Jesus saw them for what they were: captives. Jews who had been harassed and possessed for years were finally being freed. **Just as the first Joshua routed out the giants in the land the "New Joshua" waged war against the kingdom of demonic forces that enslaved the people for centuries**.

As Jesus started gaining a massive following He helped the people so much that they attempted to "take Him by force and make Him King." The Lord would have none of it. Why? Because **the people did not want Him for who He was they only wanted Him for what He could do**. They enjoyed the stories He told although "in hearing they did not understand", they enjoyed the miracles although seeing, "they did not perceive." They **thought** they wanted Him as King but He knew that they were not willing to be His subjects. (Pawson) The people were bent on nationalist ideals and they; as the Israel in the wilderness before them, were not ready to enter into the promised Kingdom of God.

Jesus proved this truth by His hard teachings:

"Large crowds were traveling with Jesus, and turning to them He said: "If anyone comes to Me and does not hate father and mother, wife and children,

brothers and sisters—yes, even their own life—such a person cannot be My disciple." (Luke 16: 25-26 NIV)

"Whoever wants to be My disciple must deny themselves and take up their cross and follow Me. For whoever wants to save their life will lose it, but whoever loses their life for Me will find it. (Matt.16:24-25 NIV)

"Jesus said to them, "Very truly I tell you, unless you eat the flesh of the Son of Man and drink His blood, you have no life in you." (John 6:53 NIV)

Slowly but surely, the crowds began to dwindle away. The people wanted a King that would overthrow the Roman government and exalt the nation of Israel not someone who commanded them to give up their lives. After all, they had been raised on the fantastic prophecies about the Messiah and Jesus was not doing things the way they envisioned the "Mighty Messiah" would. The numbers got so small that one time Jesus asked His main twelve disciples if they were going to leave Him as well! The men assured Jesus that they would never leave Him and at this He told them, 'get your wallets, pack your bags, get your swords and grab a coat; what was written about me must be fulfilled…' (Luke 22:36 paraphrased) The disciples must have thought, "Finally! The Kingdom is going to be restored to Israel." Indeed, it would be but not as they thought.

Jesus led the men up to Jerusalem and culminated His ministry by His greatest work up until then; He allowed Himself to be murdered.

Chapter 11

No Cross, No Crown

(Christ Carrying the Cross 1590-1595)
El Greco

The disciples must have been perplexed. How could Jesus get their hopes up and then... die? Things simply made no sense. It wasn't until three days later that the full scope of the King's work began to come into view. When the women who followed Jesus went to His tomb they were met by angels.

"In their fright the women bowed down with their faces to the ground, but the men said to them, "Why do you look for the living among the dead? He is not here; **He has risen!** *Remember how He told you, while He was still with you in Galilee: 'The Son of Man must be delivered over to the hands of sinners, be crucified and on the third day be raised again.' "Then they remembered His words."* (Luke 24:5-8 NIV)

What exciting news! **Jesus was alive!** During His ministry He demonstrated that He had power over demons, sickness and even nature but now His resurrection meant that He power over death too. When He appeared to His disciples they must have been both completely exhilarated and deathly afraid. As He began to teach them again His topic was none other than... **the Kingdom of God.** The Lord simply picked up where He had left off. (Acts 1:3)

The disciples later came to realize this; **Jesus was not just the King of Israel but He was also the mediator of a new covenant between God and humanity.** He was the high priest that Moses saw in Heaven back on Mount Sinai. He was the true sacrificial lamb that the Levitical priests were replicating every time they performed their duties. And, it was Jesus, the only Son of the Father, which Abraham's sacrifice was pointing to when he almost offered Isaac on Mount Moriah.

Before Jesus could assume the throne He had to complete His priestly work first. God used the prophet Isaiah over 600 years before Jesus was born to give the most detailed prophecy about the Messiah's sacrifice:

*"See, My Servant will act wisely; He will be raised and lifted up and highly exalted. Just as there were many who were appalled at Him — His appearance was so disfigured beyond that of any human being and His form marred beyond human likeness— so **He will sprinkle many nations**, and kings will shut their mouths because of Him. For what they were not told, they will see, and what they have not heard, they will understand."(Isaiah 52:13-15 NIV)*

*"Who has believed our message and to whom has **the Arm of the Lord** been revealed? He (the Son) grew up before Him (the Father) like a tender shoot, and like a root out of dry ground. He had no beauty or majesty to attract us to Him, nothing in His appearance that we should desire Him. He was despised and rejected by mankind, a man of suffering, and familiar with pain. Like one from whom people hide their faces He was despised, and we held Him in low esteem. Surely **He took up our pain and bore our suffering**, yet we considered Him punished by God, stricken by Him, and afflicted. But **He was pierced for our transgressions, He was crushed for our iniquities; the punishment that brought us peace was on Him, and by His wounds we are healed**. We all, like sheep, have gone astray, each of us has turned to our own way; and **the Lord has laid on Him the iniquity of us all**. He was oppressed and afflicted, yet he did not open His mouth; He was led like **a lamb to the slaughter**, and as **a sheep** before its shearers is silent, so He did not open His mouth. By oppression and judgment He was taken away. Yet who of*

his generation protested? For He was cut off from the land of the living; **for the transgression of My people He was punished.** *He was assigned a grave with the wicked and with the rich in His death, though He had done no violence, nor was any deceit in His mouth. Yet it* **was the Lord's will to crush Him and cause Him to suffer,** *and though* **the Lord makes His life an offering for sin,** *He will see His offspring and prolong His days, and the will of the Lord will prosper in His hand. After He has suffered, He will see the light of life and be satisfied; by His knowledge* **my righteous servant will justify many,** *and* **He will bear their iniquities.** *Therefore I will give Him a portion among the great, and He will divide the spoils with the strong, because He poured out His life unto death, and was numbered with the transgressors. For* **He bore the sin of many, and made intercession for the transgressors.** *"*

(Isaiah   53 NIV)

After Jesus rose from the dead the smoke of prophetic mystery began to clear. No wonder when John the Baptist saw Him coming he outburst, "Behold the Lamb of God who takes away the sins of the world!" **Jesus was the perfect merger of both King and Priest.** The nation of Israel never had a king who officially functioned as a priest as well. The two offices were separate. The one focused on governing the people through administrative duties whereas the other interceded on behalf of the people to God. Jesus was destined to do both.

God foretold of this monumental event in great detail through the Prophet Zechariah saying,

"Take the silver and gold and **make a crown, and set it on the head of the high priest,** *Joshua son of Jozadak. Tell him this is what the Lord Almighty says:*

75

*'Here is the man whose name is the Branch, and He will branch out from His place and build the temple of the Lord. It is He who will build the temple of the Lord, and He will be clothed with majesty and will sit and rule on His throne. And **He will be a priest on His throne.** And there will be **harmony between the two**." (Zech. 6:10-13 NIV)*

If the reader recalls, this is now the second time that the blessed name of Joshua was used. In this instance, that was the name of the high priest in office during Zechariah's time period. As we discussed in chapter 8, the name Joshua is actually Yeshua which means the salvation of God. This high priest had the exact name of Jesus Himself.

Finally, it was foretold in the Psalms that the Messiah would be a priest forever after the order of Melchizedek. So who was this "Melchizedek"?

*"This Melchizedek was **king** of Salem and **priest** of God Most High. He met Abraham returning from the defeat of the kings and blessed him, and Abraham gave him a tenth of everything. First, the name Melchizedek means "**king of righteousness**"; then also, "king of Salem" means "**king of peace.**" Without father or mother, without genealogy, without beginning of days or end of life, **resembling the Son of God**, he remains a priest forever." (Heb. 7:1-3 NIV)*

Many Jewish leaders did not see how the two offices could ever be reconciled in the service of one man. The work of the suffering servant and the reigning king were so different that some sages even theorized that Israel would have two different messiahs. Through the high priestly work of Christ the lowly disciples now had the answer to share with the world.

76

Part II

The Kingdom that Is...

Chapter 12

The Birth of a New Nation

(Pentecost 1618-1620)
Anthony Van Dyke

After being rejected by His nation **Jesus moved into the next phase of the Kingdom plan.** The nation of Israel turned on Jesus and made it known that they would not have Him reign as their King. He was given into the hands of Imperial Rome for execution. Jesus came to His own Jewish people but they did not receive Him but to all who did accept Him He later give them the power to become "Sons of God."

He told the Pharisees a parable and then made this serious statement:

> *"Have you never read in the Scriptures: 'The stone the builders rejected has become the cornerstone; the Lord has done this, and it is marvellous in our eyes'? "Therefore I tell you that **the Kingdom of God will be taken away from you and given to a people who will produce its fruit.**" (Matt. 21: 42-43 NIV)*

What new nation was He referring to? **The answer is the Church! The Church of Jesus Christ is not a religious organization but rather a nation.** The Lord stated that He would build His Church upon the foundational truth of His divine Kingship. He assured His followers that the "gates of Hell" itself could not prevail against the nation that He was going to build. The King was going to use His royal sovereignty to do "a new thing" on the earth. The disciples later came to see that this new nation was special because it's family ties were not due to a common ethnicity but rather a common Spirit. The national Jews were one body because they all came from Abraham but **this new ecclesial nation was one body comprised of members from several different nationalities.**

79

Paul the Apostle wrote:

*"Just as a body, though one, has many parts, but all its many parts form one body, so it is with Christ. For **we were all baptized by one Spirit so as to form one body**—whether Jews or Gentiles, slave or free—and we were all given the one Spirit to drink. Even so the body is not made up of one part but of many."*

(1 Cor. 12:12-14 NIV)

The same way that natural Israel became a nation so did the Church. Consider the parallels:

National Phenomena	Israel	Church
Called Out (Ekklesia)	Of Egypt	Of Slavery to Sin
Baptism	Passed through Red Sea unto Moses	Personal Baptism as the Lord Commands into Christ
Communion	Manna from Heaven	The Eucharist of the Body of Christ
Spiritual Drink	Water from the Rock	The Wine of Communion which represents the blood of Christ
The Laws	Moses at Sinai	Christ's Sermon on the Mount
The Wilderness	Land between Egypt and Land of Canaan	Time between Freedom and the Revealed Kingdom

Warfare	*Against Giants*	*Against Demons*
Priesthood	*The tribe of Levi*	*All Citizens*
Rulers	*The tribe of Judah*	*All Citizens*
Prophets	*Certain Individuals*	*All Citizens*

So, God the Father kept His promise to faithful Abraham after all, "Behold I will make you a father of many nations." Because Jesus Christ is the promised Seed from the linage of Abraham and we are begotten by the Spirit through Christ we have been grafted into the covenant as well. It does not matter which physical nation we are from. Once we are baptized into the body of Christ we become a part of the "one new man" that the Lord established.

The challenge now for any believer who has been born again by the Spirit to is to understand, believe and live in accordance with this truth. When Jesus, The King, speaks His Word constitutes law in the Kingdom of God. Who can undo what God Himself has done? Who can change what God has fixed? In His earthly ministry Jesus redefined forever what it meant to be a true family. He said My "mother or brother are those who do the will of My Father." These words were not poetic. They are Kingdom law. They were not semantics. They are Kingdom law. They were not suggestions. **They are Kingdom law**.

To be clear, **the Church of Jesus Christ is not the Kingdom of God** either. The first is a body of people whereas the second is a system of government. The Church is the nation that has been granted access to the government of Heaven. In exchange, this nation must conform to the wishes of the King and serve as His ambassadors in the current world-system. How could Jesus be so sure that this nation could "produce the fruit of righteousness" that the Kingdom of God expects when all others have failed before? The answer is that He would equip the Church with something that no other nation ever had before. **The entire nation would be baptised in the Holy Spirit.** This is the same Spirit that empowered Jesus during His earthly ministry. It is the power that carried Him through to victory.

*"When the day of Pentecost came, they were all together in one place. Suddenly a sound like the blowing of a violent wind came from heaven and filled the whole house where they were sitting. They saw what seemed to be tongues of fire that separated and came to rest on each of them. **All of them were filled with the Holy Spirit** and began to speak in other tongues as the Spirit enabled them."* (Acts 2:1-4 NIV)

The Holy Spirit was back! His glorious presence filled the men and women until they overflowed with joy. Together they discovered that the manifestation of the Kingdom of God on earth is "love, joy and peace in the Holy Spirit." In that moment, nothing else mattered. All of the personal, national and physical differences the people had melted away in the fire of God's presence. The Church would go on to do all they could to keep the unity of the Spirit in the bond of peace. Jesus knew that this nation would not fail because **He Himself would be doing the works of God through them** by the power of the Holy Spirit

Chapter 13

Spoiling the Strongman's House

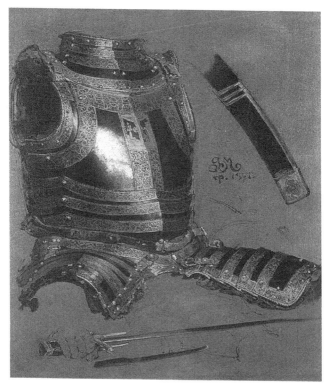

(The Armory of Stefan Batory 1872)
Jan Matejko

Christ the King declared war against the demonic powers. He came directly against Satan, the prince of darkness, in order to break the powers that were used to enslaved men to sinful desires.

Jesus Christ, the true Joshua, led the charge into the enemy's camp and He commanded the spiritual warriors to follow Him in. On the cross, the powers of Hell clashed with the power of Heaven and lost. The Kingdom of light tore an unamendable hole in the veil of darkness which covered the Earth.

Jesus said,

*"**Now is the prince of this world cast out** and when I am lifted up I will draw all men to Myself..."*
(John 12:31-32 NIV)

The Apostle Paul later expounded:

*"Jesus **disarmed the powers and authorities**, He made **a public spectacle** of them, **triumphing over them by the cross**." (Col. 2:15 NIV)*

*"God the Father's intent was that now, **through the church, the manifold wisdom of God should be made known to the rulers and authorities in the heavenly realms**, according to His eternal purpose that He accomplished in Christ Jesus our Lord." (Eph. 3:10 NIV)*

Jesus was raiding the Devil's camp and reclaiming captives for the Kingdom of God. He used an analogy that explained exactly what was taking place:

*"...If **I drive out demons by the finger of God, then the Kingdom of God has come upon you**. When a strong man, fully armed, guards his own house, his*

*possessions are safe. But when **Someone Stronger** attacks and overpowers him, He takes away the armor in which the man trusted and divides up his plunder...Whoever is not with Me is against Me, and whoever does not gather with Me scatters."*

(Luke 11:19-23 NIV)

Here, the Lord offers great insight about Satan's kingdom. He likens it to armor. When we explore this imagery many things are revealed. Essentially, armor is for battle. It covers the wearer and makes them much stronger than they really are. It also makes the wearer appear a lot more fearsome and formidable than they otherwise would. It is usually magnificently decorated. Each piece is intelligently fashioned to interlock with the others in order to create a network of impenetrable hide. It is used is for both attack and defense all while distracting the opponent in combat.

With this in mind, we can now pose the question, "what is Satan's armor?" I submit to you that **the armor in the kingdom of darkness is the systems of this world.** Satan and his minions burrow in the armor of the economic, social, political and religious systems and use them as machinery to grind victims en masse. The millions of victims who are trapped by these systems become victimizers themselves.

Paul points out to the Corinthian Church that:

> *"Satan, **the god of this age** (world-system) has **blinded the minds** of unbelievers so that they cannot see the light of the Gospel that displays the glory of Christ, who is the image of God."*

(2 Cor. 4:4 NLT)

He also noted in Ephesians:

"You used to live in sin just like the rest of the world obeying **the Devil-the commander of the powers in the unseen world.** *He is the spirit at work in the hearts of those who refuse to obey God."*

(Eph.2:2 NLT)

The rivets in Satan's armor are people who: love money, love power, love pleasure and love themselves. These are the ones he empowers in this world's system to rule in the kingdom of darkness. They attract the allegiance of like-minded slaves by luring them with a common lust. Men of like passions come and their resources are added to the lot. As the Devil's treasury is increased, his armor is fortified, his soldiers are sworn in and his kingdom is expanded. With great fury he resists his kingdom being ransacked. He and his demons hold out against the influence of the Holy Spirit at all cost. The reason is because **once these spiritual "strong men" are exposed their armor can be stripped and the material reclaimed for God's purpose!**

Paul cautioned the Ephesian Church to be prepared to battle against demonic forces:

"Be strong in the Lord and in His mighty power. Put on all of God's armor so that you will be able to stand firm against all strategies of the Devil. For **we are not fighting against flesh-and-blood enemies, but against evil rulers and authorities of the unseen world, against mighty powers in this dark world, and against evil spirits in the heavenly places…"** *(Eph. 6:10-12 NLT)*

The people of the Kingdom of God have been commissioned to move out and invade the darkness with the light. We are to go and set the captives free. Once these enslaved people are taken out of the old world-system and come into the light they bring all their

86

resources along with them. Their bodies, their gifts, their relationships, their time, their past and their purpose are all redeemed for King Jesus' use. Nothing is wasted.

Chapter 14

Victory through Sacrifice

(The Martyrdom of St. Matthew 1599-1600)
Michelangelo Merisi Da Caravaggio

Jesus' death was not just atonement but it was also an investment. He taught the disciples that 'except a Seed fall into ground and die then it would not be able to reproduce.' (John 12:24) Jesus was a Seed packed with eternal life and He knew that He needed to give His life in order to be the "firstborn in a harvest of many brothers and sisters." When He died, the Priestly-King extended His Kingdom thousands of times over by raising slaves to the status of divine nobility.

Jesus was the new and final Adam. He became the progenitor of a completely new race of enlightened people. He then commanded His new family members to go into all of the world-system with the news of the Kingdom of God and make disciples of all nations. In other words, He told His brethren "go and do what I have done here in Israel all over the world." Not only would they be successful but those who believe would do even greater works than He himself had done. In addition to the instructions, **Jesus gave His Kingdom citizens power**. "Heal the sick, raise the dead... tread upon serpents and scorpions and over all the powers of darkness." (Matt.10:8) With this distribution of dunamis power the King rightly focused the citizens of the Kingdom on the source of the world's problems and not merely the symptoms the powers of darkness create.

Jesus has always expected the believers to go out and proclaim His Kingship now. (Acts 17:7) He never said the mission would be easy. In fact, He warned the Church **that the kingdoms of this world are hostile to the Kingdom of God**.

He prepared the disciples saying,

"*If the world hates you, keep in mind that it hated Me first. If you belonged to the world, it would love you as its own. As it is, you do not belong to the world, but I have chosen you out of the world. That is why the world hates you. Remember what I told you: 'A servant is not greater than his Master.' If they persecuted Me, they will persecute you also. If they obeyed My teaching, they will obey yours also. They will treat you this way because of My name, for they do not know the One who sent Me...*" *(John 15:18-21 NIV)*

In chapter 1 of this book I explained that the term "world" is different from the term "earth" in the Bible. The earth is the land whereas the world is system that governs the resources of the land. The Kingdom citizen brings God's alternative government to every area of life. **When the believer comes to the people who are under the control of this world-system those people are naturally offended.** They resent the idea that all they have belongs to another especially if that person is Jesus Christ! Some of these men who love darkness protect their possessions and desires with great fervor. They use anything to continue indulgence: human reason, legislation, group alliances, money, lies, propaganda, fear, and if all else fails sheer violence.

On the contrary, **God's Kingdom people represent a government that is not dominated by human desires or material possessions.** The Kingdom citizens do not love money, power, pleasure or self. They are dead to the world-system but alive to God. They are integrated yet sanctified; immerse yet Holy. They are under orders to do everything as unto the Lord and their entire lives become a testament to the light of

God. These are the people who are the "Salt of the Earth" and the "Light of the World."

Once the spirit of darkness in the children of disobedience is confronted by the Children of Light it becomes antagonistic towards them. The animosity grows so much that the people of this world's system seek to attack the Kingdom citizens. It is in the fire of persecution that the yeast of the Kingdom of God expands! **Christian Martyrs have tread this rough and narrow way for centuries.**

Here is how it works:

Those under the Devil's power attack the saint and he does not resist. He turns the other cheek. He blesses when cursed. He loves when hated. He gives when he is taken advantage of. He demonstrates God at his core and at once the face of the Devil is exposed in his adversaries.

` The onlookers see who each person really is in the fires of persecution. As fiery coals of generosity are heaped on the heads of the antagonist **the very thing that Satan meant for evil God uses for the greatest good.** The attackers thought they had taken the life of the saint but in all actuality he wilfully laid it down just as his Master did. The Kingdom citizen is sown as a seed into a fallen world to die and as a result he bears the fruit of many more Sons and Daughters. The wisdom of God is exalted because in this painful process He uses the furious devils to bring glory to Himself. To all it becomes evident that **the kingdom of darkness grows through selfishness but the Kingdom of Light grows through sacrifice**.

Chapter 15

The Invisible Kingdom

(Sermon on the Mount 1880)
Henrik Olrik

Now is a good time to bring the conversation of the Kingdom of God into our modern day context. In doing so the first question someone might have is this, **"If Jesus is King right now then where is He?"** The answer is: **He is in Heaven**. He is there enthroned at the right hand of God the Father in glory and power. His purpose there is threefold: to intercede on behalf of His followers to the Father, to establish residence for His followers that will soon be with Him in Heaven and to continually pour out the oil of the Holy Spirit on Kingdom citizens.

If He is in Heaven then how does He rule Earth? **Jesus is ruling right now by His Spirit.** Remember the earth is the Lord's and the bounty that comes from it. In fact all of creation is held together by the power of His Spirit. The only power that Satan truly has at this time is the power of deception. This is why he is called the prince of the power of the "air". (Eph.2) **The Devil's immaterial power works indirectly through influence not directly through substance.** Hence, he has created several false world-systems that capitalize on sinful desires but the truth is his kingdom is on its way out and a new day is dawning. The Evil One has been working hard to keep people under his control until this very hour but nothing can stop the inevitable establishment of God's Kingdom on earth.

Another way Jesus is reigning is in the hearts and minds of people who are filled with His Spirit. One might think that this strategy is inconsequential but the truth is it is absolute genius. Once the Lord saves a person's soul He then reclaims their life and resources for His Kingdom. This means that everything that person touches: work, home, possessions, family, money, and community become subject to the Holy Spirit that is resident in that person. Until this day God has been spoiling the spiritual kingdom of "Egypt" every time one of His Sons comes out and brings their gold with them. Just as the gold of Israel was used to build the tabernacle so the resources of the redeemed are used to advance the Kingdom of God.

The Kingdom of God is invisible yet its felt impact is steadily growing. In an effort to clarify how an invisible kingdom can hold such power I encourage you to take a moment to consider your own national government. Here are two questions I would like you as the reader to consider. First, when have you ever actually laid eyes on a government official? Isn't it true that for the most part these people move and operate in secrecy?

Second, are you aware of the patriotic spirit in your own country? If you wonder about this simply talk to a veteran or a police officer and have them inform you. They will tell you that without question they are under charge of the government and they have an overwhelming sense of duty to protect and to serve no matter the cost. They embody what one would call the "spirit of patriotism". It is this spirit of brotherhood that makes military orders fraternal organizations because its members are bound together for the "common good".

Now, if patriotism is real and government officials can rule through legislation even if we don't see them in person is it really a strange thing to think that the King of the Earth is ruling from Heaven? Christ the King has His own process of governing the world through people who have pledged their allegiance to Him and embody the Spirit of heavenly patriotism.

All of these concepts sketch out a simple truth: **the Kingdom of Heaven is all around us but it is**

invisible! It is currently a spiritual domain that exists in the realm of the heavenly places. Count up the facts: If the King is ruling from Heaven, His citizens are all around us, they are filled with His Spirit and we all live on His property then the Kingdom of God is all around us. It is hidden in plain sight. Few people realize this and even fewer live like it but it is the truth nonetheless. Take Jesus' words on the matter.

He explained to the Pharisees that the Kingdom of God was right in their midst but they failed to detect it:

*"Once, on being asked by the Pharisees when the Kingdom of God would come, Jesus replied, **"The coming of the Kingdom of God is not something that can be observed**, nor will people say, 'Here it is,' or 'There it is,' because the **Kingdom of God is in your midst (among you)."*** (Luke 17:20-21 NIV)

He said this because He Himself was right in front of them filled with the Spirit of Heaven but they did not realize it. **Wherever the King is there the Kingdom is**.

Jesus even explained to a leader named Nicodemus how to enter into the Kingdom:

*"Jesus replied, "Very truly I tell you, **no one can see the Kingdom of God unless they are born again.**""How can someone be born when they are old?" Nicodemus asked. "Surely they cannot enter a second time into their mother's womb to be born!" Jesus answered, "Very truly I tell you, no one can enter the Kingdom of God unless they are born of water and the Spirit. Flesh gives birth to flesh, but the Spirit gives birth to spirit. You should not be surprised at My saying, 'You must be born again.' The wind blows wherever it*

pleases. You hear its sound, but you cannot tell where it comes from or where it is going. So it is with everyone born of the Spirit." (John 3:3-8 NIV)

Jesus taught His disciples that He is the doorway that leads to eternal life. No one could enter into the Kingdom of God without coming to Him in repentance and then being spiritually translated out of the kingdom of darkness into the Kingdom of Light. Any genuinely born again person will tell you that they are "not the same person" they used to be. Something special happened to them that is beyond a mere conversion into a religion. They have stepped into the light. They may have the same name, body and earthly identity but they are different. It is these spiritual people that no longer belong to this world-system but are now citizens of the Kingdom of God. This explains why they feel out of place in this world; they are no longer "of it."

Jesus did not leave His followers without comfort in this world-system but He gave them His Holy Spirit. He conferred on them His Kingdom and said "where two or three are gathered together in My name, I am in the midst."(Matt.18:20) This is good news because wherever the King is there the Kingdom is.

Chapter 16

The Local Church Mindset vs. the Kingdom Mindset

(Ufton Church 1809-1869)
Thomas Baker

Where does the local church fit within the context of the Kingdom? In order to answer this question properly we have to correct a major error. **The "church" is not a building!** The church is the nation of born again Kingdom citizens. This distinction is critical since wrong ideas lead to wrong ideology. (Munroe) Such inaccuracy must be corrected at once because the damage it has already done is enormous. The places where the church meets can be called: meeting houses, sanctuaries, temples, homes or any other name the Holy Spirit designates but they should not be called churches. By making this fatal mistake people believe that "church" is a dusty place that elderly people go to on Sundays after they're too tired to party anymore. The idea portrays a mere religious activity and not a daily reality.

The old traditional church mindset is one of a social club. People come in, dress up, show off and escape the troubles of the world for a few hours. This escapism concept is completely unhealthy and it is not what the King had in mind at all. Many of these organizations become self-absorbed and grow stale as soon as the fiery visionary who founded the place dies. Worse yet, church members build doctrines and denominations around their memory. Do the terms Lutheran or Calvinist ring a bell? These denominations along with the over 4,000 others are nothing more than sects which reinforce splits in the body of Christ. They are championed by people who do not see the global Kingdom of God worldwide but they are blinded by their loyalty to a religious party. No doubt, there are some sincere people in Christendom who identify with each one of these denominations but the truth is before the Kingdom can fully come these petty classifications need to go.

Listen to how the Apostle Paul addressed this same problem among the Corinthians:

*"I appeal to you, brothers and sisters, in the name of our Lord Jesus Christ, that all of you **agree with one another in what you say** and that there be **no divisions** among you, but that you be **perfectly united in mind and thought**. My brothers and sisters, some from Chloe's household have informed me that there are quarrels among you. What I mean is this: One of you says, "I follow Paul"; another, "I follow Apollos"; another, "I follow Cephas"; still another, "I follow Christ." **Is Christ divided?** "* (1 Cor. 1:10-13 NIV)

The Kingdom mindset is global. It tears down walls of division and helps the body of Christ unite under one banner. It aides in getting Christian disciples to identify with one another as family members working for a common cause. In addition to being global, it is also eternal which indicates that the saints throughout history are to be viewed as living family members rather than untouchable corpses that belong in reliquaries. The Kingdom of God eliminates the need for any other denominational or national descriptors for believers. Hyphenated titles such as Haitian-Church or Spanish-Church or Korean-Church or English-Church or Messianic-Church or this or that denominational Church are rendered useless. In the Kingdom of God there are no grounds for superiority, inferiority, isolation or separation. Denominations encourage the "us" and "them" mentality whereas the Kingdom mindset views these things as an offence to the cross of Christ. It was by the cross that the King Himself abolished all divisions in His Kingdom.

Sanctuaries are to be places where the Holy Spirit and the Word of God are the main focus. This is not to say they should function like the embarrassing caricatures that many "Pentecostal" churches display nor should they be the opposite cold boring cemeteries many "orthodox" churches resemble. The meeting houses are just that; meeting houses. They can and should be everywhere including in the homes of the believers. They are places where life among new family members is lived, resources are shared and everyone is taught. They should look a lot like healthy homes. People do not pretend in their homes instead they find freedom being themselves among they ones they love.

Finally, **sanctuaries must serve as lighthouses in the community.** That is why they are there. The sanctuaries where the King's citizens gather are holy places. This is not because they are special in and of themselves; they're not. It is because the King's people are holy. Where there are holy people and the Holy Spirit there is the Kingdom of God. It is only right to say that these small colonies of Heaven on Earth must be healing centers for the communities around them. The hands of the saints are the ones to help the lost world not the welfare programs of a secular government. The meeting house is the place where the Kingdom citizens gather to be refreshed by one another in the Holy Spirit. The idea is a lot like a tired athlete who goes to the locker room to regain his strength. No athlete would think his locker room experience was equal to playing the sport but often many Christians think church attendance is the full extent of their Christian life. They even call this activity going to "service."

We are not merely "church members" we are citizens of God's Kingdom.

100

Chapter 17

Practical Kingdom Life for Today

(The Rush Hour in New York City 1900)
Colin Campbell Cooper

There are many ways **a believer in Jesus Christ can and should function in the Kingdom of God today**. I have four recommendations that will be of great practical value. The first thing I would like to recommend is to simply **be sure to understand the overarching Biblical narrative correctly.** The Bible is about God establishing His Kingdom on earth through people. When we lose sight of this things get confusing and all sorts of doctrines spring up. Remember, **Jesus only spoke of this one message publicly**. Every parable was meant to explain Kingdom truth and every miracle was meant to display Kingdom power. The vigilant believer must search the Old and New Testament scriptures to find the common thread of the Kingdom in both.

As Jesus said,

*"Therefore every teacher of the law who has become a disciple in the Kingdom of Heaven is like the owner of a house who brings out of his storeroom **new treasures as well as old.**" (Matt. 13:52 NIV)*

The next thing that every believer in the Messiah, Jesus, should do is begin to **respect Him as King**. I am aware that we all love Jesus very much. He has saved us from Hell and we owe everything to Him but we cannot allow our personal relationship to take precedence over His Lordship. We have to respect Him, His power, His word, and His will as the King of the Earth and the Lord of our lives. I stress this point because the knowledge of the Kingdom of God is not just theory or theology but something to practice daily. Every day and in every way we should do only what honors the King. Paul rightful taught, "whatever you do in word or deed do all to the glory of God."(Col. 3:17) This mindset keeps us in constant communion with the Lord.

I encourage the reader to go back to the gospels and study Jesus' words again carefully. **His words say what they say and mean what they say**; do not be fooled by the thousands of scholars who "add or detract" from the King's words in an attempt to make His teaching more palatable for a contemporary audience. They should be treated with the utmost respect as eternal law not moral suggestion.

Thirdly, the believer must seek to be filled with the Holy Spirit continually. The Kingdom of God is only truly realized in the presence of the Holy Spirit. So many western churches are locked in religious routine that there is no room for the Spirit on the program. These churches either create emotional experiences using lights and melodies or avoid the topic of the Holy Spirit all together. Most Christians think they have been filled with the Holy Spirit because they have been born again or had an emotional moment in a church service. This is not the case and we must be honest about it. Worst yet, there are even doctrines such as the doctrine of "cessation" that teaches the gifts of the Holy Spirit have ceased! Such Pharisaical leaven is taught by big names from behind the pulpit and it has created a powerless church. Do not be deceived; Jesus Christ is the same yesterday, today and forever. One more word here. Please bear in mind, if we are going to seek to be filled with the Holy Spirit we must prepare the way for Him in our hearts. **The continuing practice of sin must be removed** and we must pursue the Lord for this most sacred gift with an undying hunger.

The apostle James spoke to believers these words:

*"Submit yourselves, then, to God. Resist the devil, and he will flee from you. Come near to God and He will come near to you. **Wash your hands, you***

103

sinners, and purify your hearts, you double-minded.
Grieve, mourn and wail. Change your laughter to
mourning and your joy to gloom. Humble yourselves
before the Lord, and He will lift you up."

(James 4:7-10 NIV)

Finally, **each Kingdom citizen should seek to establish the physical expression of Kingdom of God where they live.** We are the ones who translate God's invisible will into the visible world. (Munroe) Just like Nehemiah commanded each Jew to rebuild the part of the wall near their house each Kingdom citizen must establish righteousness where they live. This requires us getting out of our "religious bubbles" and seeing the needs all around us.

Here are a few questions that should get you going:

- *What effort would you give on your job if you believed Jesus was you auditor?*
- *Do you work to fulfill your purpose or to collect a pay check?*
- *How are you really supposed to be using your gifts to advance the Kingdom?*
- *What sinful movies are in your house right now that must go?*
- *Whose phone number do you need to delete right now?*
- *What websites have you visited this week that have short circuited your anointing?*
- *How many homeless people are in your city?*
- *What is in place for battered women near you?*
- *What humanitarian organization exists near your church?*
- *What is the poverty level in your state?*
- *What hospital near you needs the most help?*

- *What school is struggling to make adequate yearly progress?*
- *What laws are up for vote that are either for or against the King's wishes?*
- *What is your church doing to combat abortion in your city?*
- *What unrighteousness should you be praying against in your professional industry?*

The Lord taught us not to wait for the harvest but look up today and see the ripe fields. People need both a word from the Lord and a helping hand. We must have wisdom on which one to lead out with first.

Part III

The Kingdom that Is to Come.

Chapter 18

The Economic Trap
(Signs of the Gathering Storm)

(Mammon and His Slave 1896)
Sascha Schneider

It is always darkest just before the dawn. The King told the believers that things would get worse before they got better and God cannot lie. We can see more now in our current era than any generation could in the past. We have advanced in travel, technology, information and commerce. There have been many wonderful advances particularly in the areas of medicine and the quality of life but there have also been many developments that reveal the worst in human nature. While I understand that many factors create social conditions, I would like to just focus on three in these next few chapters that are signposts pointing to the Lord's return.

The first glaring sign that the Day of the Lord's return is near is the growth of **the world wide economy**. This world-system has always thrived on commerce so the idea is nothing new. What is new however is the speed at which transactions are conducted. Through the advent of the internet transactions are conducted faster than the speed of light. People in the west purchase goods from sellers on the other side of the earth with the click of a button. This is not really a problem; in fact, the concept of a global market is a good thing. What is alarming is that the whole process is not done using real "hard" money but rather a digital system of zeros and ones. This means that **whoever controls the infrastructure that is in charge of "digital accounting" controls the economy.**

Big world banks have figured this out long ago and they have been craftily using our commercial appetites to strengthen the chains of debt that bind us. Most national economies around the world are completely unbalanced. The amount of debt that the each country has can never be paid by its gross domestic product (GDP) and this can cause the currency of that nation to inflate. I do not mean to lose the reader in jargon here but I am building the foundation for a crucial point. The Bible is clear, "the borrower is a slave to the lender." (Prov. 22:7) This means that everyone in an indebted nation is subject to slavery in some form whether they realize it or not. It may come in the form of higher taxes or stagnant wages but it is the truth.

Such economic conditions set the perfect stage for a **"one world currency."** The Bible often uses allegorical terms to describe things so that the reader has to look beyond what is said in order to capture the meaning of the text. The world economic system is known as the system of "Babylon" in the book of Revelations. It is prophesied that in the last days that no one will be able to buy or sell (participate in the economy) if they do not take the "Mark of the Beast" in their hands or foreheads. Such a concept may have sounded far-fetched in John's day but we are now one major economic crisis away from it become a reality in ours. Between digital banking, barcode scanners and fingerprint identification to access everything it seems as if the population is being conditioned for this next phase of governmental control.

Jesus' position on money was very clear:

*"**No one can serve two masters.** Either you will hate the one and love the other, or you will be devoted to the one and despise the other. You cannot serve both God and money."(Matt.6:24 NIV)*

*"Do not worry, saying, 'What shall we eat?' or 'What shall we drink?' or 'What shall we wear?' **For the pagans run after all these things** (the minds of the heathen are dominated by these things), and your*

109

heavenly Father knows that you need them. But seek first His Kingdom and His righteousness, and all these things will be given to you as well." (Matt. 6:31-33 NIV)

Paul went on to teach Timothy:

*"... **The love of money is a root of all kinds of evil.** Some people, eager for money, have wandered from the faith and pierced themselves with many griefs."*
(1 Tim. 6:10 NIV)

The people who are still in the kingdom of darkness are money worshippers. This is a harsh statement but it is deduced from what the Lord and the Apostles taught. The two major motivations for all of mankind are either the love of God or the love of money and no one can serve both. In the conditions that I have sketched out with reference to the global economy it easy to see how "normal people" could become vicious and violent if anyone taught them what Jesus taught His disciples back in Judea.

He said:

*"Do not be afraid, little flock, for your Father has been pleased to give you the Kingdom. **Sell your possessions and give to the poor.** Provide purses for yourselves that will not wear out, a treasure in Heaven that will never fail, where no thief comes near and no moth destroys. For where your treasure is, there your heart will be also."* (Luke 12:32-34 NIV)

When the Holy Spirit filled the believers in the book of Acts they all entered into the Kingdom of Heaven. They were never the same after that. They whole meaning of life for them had shifted to a heavenly focus instead of an earthly one. In light of this, they sold

110

their possessions to provide for each other's needs. They were not forced or persuaded to do it but rather they did it joyfully! God confirmed this way of life because there was no lack among them.

Here's a snapshot of life among the first Kingdom citizens:

"They devoted themselves to the apostles' teaching and to fellowship, to the breaking of bread and to prayer. Everyone was filled with awe at the many wonders and signs performed by the apostles. ***All the believers were together and had everything in common. They sold property and possessions to give to anyone who had need.*** *Every day they continued to meet together in the temple courts. They broke bread in their homes and ate together with glad and sincere hearts, praising God and enjoying the favor of all the people. And the Lord added to their number daily those who were being saved."* (Acts 2:42-47 NIV)

When these two views of material possessions are placed side by side the contrasts become evident. The Lord will always take care of His Kingdom citizens but economic strain will continue to be a factor in the days leading up to the King's arrival.

Chapter 19

Media Control of the Masses
(Signs of the Gathering Storm)

(The Laughing Fool 1500)
Jacob Cornelisz Van Oostsan

Another sign that is precursor to the Lord's return is the swift rise of media control in the twentieth and twenty-first centuries. Our modern culture is flooded with: television, radio, the internet, cell phones, movies, music, videogames, magazines, book, social media, entertainment venues, news outlets and more! The information glut is staggering.

Daniel prophesied about the last days saying:

"Those who are wise will shine like the brightness of the heavens, and those who lead many to righteousness, like the stars for ever and ever. But you, Daniel, roll up and seal the words of the scroll until the time of the end. **Many will go here and there and knowledge shall increase.***"* *(Dan.12:3-4 NIV)*

The fact that we now have equal access to knowledge is a great thing but **not all knowledge is "good"** for us. Recall in the Garden of Eden how God forbade Adam to eat from the tree of "the knowledge of good and evil." Some information is evil and it is better for humanity if it is not explored. God did however provide Adam many options for exploration and they were all good. All too often we are fixated on the one restricted tree in the garden and fail to see the thousands that were open for the taking.

The main issue with all of this mass media production is that the industries behind them are driven by the love of money. The producers seldom care about the welfare of the human psyche; instead they are motivated by profits and ratings. Most media companies cater to the recalcitrant desires of human sin in hopes of increasing the appetite for debauchery in society. The more views the company gets the more they can charge for commercial advertisement. The whole thing is a system of control.

Finally, apart from the motivation of money there are entities that have a much more malicious agenda in mind. They have found out how effective media is as a propaganda tool and with it they push ideas on the impressionable masses. A famous political activist named Andrew Fletcher made the following statement, "Let me make the songs of a nation, and I care not who makes its laws." Fletcher knew what every media producer knows, **first art reflects life and then life reflects art.** That said, many ungodly concepts such as homosexuality, abortion, racism and promiscuity have been feed to the minds of the people in both overt and covert ways. Those who advocate for such ways of life are against the Kingdom of God and fight all who seek a righteous world.

King Jesus made it clear:

"Not everyone who says to Me, Lord, Lord, shall enter into the Kingdom of Heaven; **but he who does the will of My Father which is in Heaven.***"*
(Matt. 7:21 NIV)

Paul follows this in stating:

*"Know ye not that **the unrighteous shall not inherit the Kingdom of God**? Be not deceived: neither fornicators, nor idolaters, nor adulterers, nor feminine men, nor abusers of themselves with mankind (men who have sex with other men), Nor thieves, nor covetous, nor drunkards, nor revilers, nor extortioners, shall inherit the Kingdom of God." (1 Cor. 6:9-10 NIV)*

*"The acts of the flesh are obvious: sexual immorality, impurity and debauchery; idolatry and witchcraft; hatred, discord, jealousy, fits of rage, selfish ambition, dissensions, factions, envy; drunkenness, orgies, and the like. I warn you, as I did before, that **those who live like this will not inherit the Kingdom of God.**"* (Gal. 5:19 NIV)

Isn't this the majority of what we see in all of mass media today? Isn't this the main content of the popular movies and music? Aren't these the basic themes of famous video game titles? What was once socially unacceptable has now become what is celebrated in society and conversely it has become socially unacceptable to speak against such vices.

Therefore, it is obvious that **this world-system is in rebellion against the Kingdom of God.**

Chapter 20

One World Government
(Signs of the Gathering Storm)

(The Tower of Babel 1500)
Hendrick van Cleve III

The final point of evidence that needs to be mentioned is that Satan is going to seek to create a false kingdom of god complete with a false messiah, a false world king and he himself will be attempt to be openly recognized as god over all of the earth. Such an idea might sound radical but our world is certainly moving in this direction. We are moving **towards a "one world government"** and many groups support the idea of globalization. The United Nations, The World Bank, The International Monetary Fund (IMF) and the ecumenical movement towards a one world religion are just a few that come to mind. In these entries alone we can see the basic components for an international governing body, monetary system and religion. No one can say for certain exactly how things will pan out as that would be much too speculative. However, I simply mention these organizations to demonstrate that **powerful leaders in our current world-system are already working on strategies of globalization.**

What does the Bible have to say about this? A lot! The Bible speaks in Revelations of three evil entities that will arise in the last days: the Dragon (Satan), the Beast (A global political machine led by the Antichrist), and the False Prophet (A false religious messiah). The Holy Spirit speaks through John in apocalyptic language to warn the believers of the coming days.

"The dragon stood on the shore of the sea. And I saw a beast coming out of the sea. It had ten horns and seven heads, with ten crowns on its horns, and on each head a blasphemous name. The beast I saw resembled a leopard, but had feet like those of a bear and a mouth like that of a lion. The dragon gave the beast his power and his throne and great authority. One of the heads of the beast seemed to have had a fatal wound, but the fatal

117

wound had been healed. The whole world was filled with wonder and followed the beast. People worshiped the dragon because he had given authority to the beast, and they also worshiped the beast and asked, "Who is like the beast? Who can wage war against it?"

"The beast was given a mouth to utter proud words and blasphemies and to exercise its authority for forty-two months. It opened its mouth to blaspheme God, and to slander His name and His dwelling place and those who live in Heaven. **It was given power to wage war against God's holy people and to conquer them.** *And it was given* **authority over every tribe, people, language and nation**. **All inhabitants of the earth will worship the beast**—*all whose names have not been written in the Lamb's book of life, the Lamb who was slain from the creation of the world."*

Whoever has ears, let them hear. "If anyone is to go into captivity,

Into captivity they will go.

If anyone is to be killed with the sword,

With the sword they will be killed.

This calls for patient endurance and faithfulness on the part of God's people." (Rev. 13:1-10 NIV)

This passage indicates that the citizen of **the Kingdom of God will be the subjects of great persecution before the King comes back**. Jesus warned that we would be hated by all men in every nation for His name's sake. While there has been much persecution against Christian believers in the past that continues to this day there has never been a time in history in which

118

all nations hated the followers of Christ at once. In a one world government system that is hostile towards the God of the Bible such persecution could become a harsh reality with the stroke of a pen. God the Father has already warned that the Beast (a political system that arise from the sea of humanity) will be given a time to fight against the saints and to kill them. Why would God allow this? The same reason He allowed Christ to die; **the blood of the righteous is a condemnation against the wicked**. (Rev. 6:10) Hence, the subsequent judgement that Christ the King will dole out on the world leaders will be completely justified.

The Apostle Paul explained, '**Through much tribulation, the saint enters into the Kingdom of God.**' (Acts 14:22) He was referring to the return of the Lord and the time in which He will set up His visible Kingdom on earth. The Lord does reign from Heaven now but soon He will reign on Earth from Jerusalem. Even in the midst of persecution the Kingdom citizen is trained to rejoice.

The Apostle came to this encouraging conclusion in his Kingdom work:

*"Who shall separate us from the love of Christ? Shall trouble or hardship or persecution or famine or nakedness or danger or sword? As it is written: "**For your sake we face death all day long; we are considered as sheep to be slaughtered.**" No, **in all these things we are more than conquerors** through Him who loved us. For I am convinced that neither death nor life, neither angels nor demons, neither the present nor the future, nor any powers, neither height nor depth, nor anything else in all creation, will be able to separate us from the love of God that is in Christ Jesus our Lord."*

(Rom. 8: 35-39 NIV)

119

Chapter 21

Yom Din; Judgment Day

(The Great Day of His Wrath 1853)
John Martin

"Behold, He cometh with clouds; and every eye shall see Him, and they also which pierced Him: and all kindreds of the earth shall wail because of Him. Even so, Amen." *(Rev. 1:7 KJV)*

The day of the Lord is going to be terrible. It will be a day like nothing humanity has ever seen. All of the Prophets, Psalms and Apostles have been warning of this day since sin entered into the world. Christ the King will finally come back and **"dash the nations into pieces with a rod of iron."** (Ps. 2)

The Old Testament Prophets warned:

Enoch, *"The Lord is coming with ten thousands of His saints to execute judgement upon all..."*
David *1000 B.C.,* *"He shall rain snares, fire and brimstone, and a horrible storm..."*
Amos *750 B.C.,* *"It will be as though a man ran from a lion only to meet a bear..."*
Isaiah *700 B.C.,* *"Go into the rock and hide in the ground from the fearful presence of the Lord"*
Zephaniah *630 B.C.,* *"Their blood will be poured out like dust ..."*
Haggai *520 B.C.,* *"I will overthrow the throne of kingdoms..."*
Zechariah *520 B.C.,* *"Their flesh shall consume away while they stand on their feet..."*

The New Testament Apostles warned:

John the Baptist *30 A.D.,* *"Flee from the wrath to come"*
Jesus *32 A.D.,* *"Every tree that does not produce good fruit will be cut down and burned..."*
Peter *34 A.D.,* *"Save yourself for this wicked and twisted generation"*

Paul 55 A.D., *"The wrath of God is revealed from heaven against all ungodliness..."*
The Hebrew's writer 63 A.D., *"the judgment of fiery indignation which would devour the adversaries..."*
Jude 70 A.D., *"The Lord is coming with ten thousands of His saints to execute judgement upon all..."*

The countdown of His-story is underway and John prophesied of His coming:

*"I saw heaven standing open and there before me was a white horse, whose rider is called Faithful and True. **With justice He judges and wages war**. His eyes are like blazing fire, and on His head are many crowns. He has a name written on Him that no one knows but He Himself. He is dressed in **a robe dipped in blood**, and His name is the Word of God. **The armies of Heaven were following Him**, riding on white horses and dressed in fine linen, white and clean. Coming out of His mouth is **a sharp sword with which to strike down the nations.** "He will rule them with an iron sceptre." He treads the winepress of the fury of the wrath of God Almighty. On His robe and on His thigh He has this name written:*

KING OF KINGS AND LORD OF LORDS

"And I saw an angel standing in the sun, who cried in a loud voice to all the birds flying in mid-air, 'Come, gather together for the great supper of God, so that you may eat the flesh of kings, generals, and the mighty, of horses and their riders, and the flesh of all people, free and slave, great and small." (Rev. 19: 11-16 NIV)

This is the event that Joel described when God said through him:

> *"I will show wonders in the heavens and on the earth, blood and fire and billows of smoke. The sun will be turned to darkness and the moon to blood before the coming of **the great and dreadful day of the Lord.**"*
>
> *(Joel 2:31-32 NIV)*

The King Himself expounds on this prophecy in great detail to His disciples:

> *"...But in those days, following that distress, 'the sun will be darkened, and the moon will not give its light; the stars will fall from the sky, and the heavenly bodies will be shaken.' "At that time people will see **the Son of Man coming in clouds with great power and glory.** And He will send His angels and gather His elect from the four winds, from the ends of the earth to the ends of the heavens." (Mark 13:24-27 NIV)*

The citizen of the Kingdom of God have been outcasts, harassed, belittled and persecuted by the nations and have returned such hate with love. The Lord has sworn to use His angels to gather them together from all over the world to protect them from this day of wrath.

> *"As the weeds are pulled up and burned in the fire, so it will be at the end of the age. The Son of Man will send out His angels, and they will weed out of His Kingdom everything that causes sin and all who do evil. They will throw them into the blazing furnace, where there will be weeping and gnashing of teeth. **Then the righteous will shine like the sun in the Kingdom of their Father.** Whoever has ears, let them hear."*
>
> *(Matt. 13: 40-43 NIV)*

Earlier in this parable the Lord explained that the "wheat" are the children of the Kingdom of God. They will be gathered together in His "barn" for safe keeping. The "weeds" on the other hand, are the children of the kingdom of darkness and they will be rooted out of the earth and burned in eternal fire. This is a frightful thought but the King is just in all He does. Who can question His will? He alone has seen **ALL** of the lies, murder, violence, hatred, greed, and evil that mankind had engaged in. **He has had to personally witness every sin since the fall of Adam so He alone knows the true extent of human depravity.**

On the Day of the Lord every human kingdom will be destroyed. Daniel prophesied that the Rock which comes from Heaven would come and crush all of the kingdoms of men. From monarchies to mansions to mobile homes, all kingdoms both great and small will come to an end. Magnificent structures that each nation was so proud of will be obliterated in an instant. No human pride will be able to revel in glory before the Lord. Leaders who ruled as tyrants over people will finally "meet their Maker" and all that men have done in the dark will be exposed to the Light of God's presence.

One might wonder, **"What about the Devil and his demons; were they not the cause of all this evil in the first place?"** The Lord will deal with the Devil and all of his unclean spirits but He also must justly judge humanity. The honest truth is that we have all chosen to sin against God. Yes, we were tempted to do so by both satanic forces and our own personal desires but everyone has made the conscious choice to "cross the line" and commit the act of sinning against God. We must own this truth. He will hold all who have not had their sins atoned for by the blood of the Lamb as the responsible party to pay for their sins. The price will be their own

124

blood instead of Jesus'. As it is written, "The soul that sins will die" and "without the shedding of blood there is no remission of sin."

When Jesus worked in His ministry on the earth over 2000 years ago He often casted out demons. We have already established in previous chapters that these demons have come from the souls of the Nephilim which inhabited the earth during the days of Noah and thereafter. On one recorded occasion a demon said something to Jesus that offered us a glimpse into their eternal fate.

*"When He arrived at the other side in the region of the Gadarenes, two demon-possessed men coming from the tombs met Him. They were so violent that no one could pass that way. "What do you want with us, Son of God?" they shouted. "**Have you come here to torture us before the appointed time?**"* (Matt.8:28-29 NIV)

This indicates that **God has set an appointed time for all of the demons to be bound and rooted out of the earth** as well. They have been the unseen forces who have excited lust, bloodshed and chaos on the earth for millennia and they will finally get there due penalty. The King will first purge the earth and weed out all the snakes of darkness before He fully establishes the Kingdom of Light. These demons said "**have you come to torture us…**" Such a statement shows that the demons are not to be pitied. They are fully aware of what they have done to humanity. They know they are guilty. They are also completely cognizant of God's impeding wrath on them yet they do not care. The demons asked for escape not forgiveness. If demons were terrified of Jesus even before He appeared in His glory, can you imagine what they all will feel when they see Him in power with all the angels of Heaven?

Now; about the Devil. John reported:

> *"I saw an angel coming down out of Heaven,*
> *having the key to the Abyss and holding in his hand a*
> *great chain. He seized the dragon, that ancient serpent,*
> *which is the devil, or **Satan**, and **bound him for a***
> ***thousand years.** He threw him into the Abyss, and*
> *locked and sealed it over him, to keep him from*
> *deceiving the nations anymore until the thousand years*
> *were ended. After that, he must be set free for a short*
> *time."*
>
> *(Rev. 20: 1-3 NIV)*

We see that the Lord will cause Satan to be bound for 1000 years as He sets up The Kingdom of Heaven on Earth. There is an interesting passage in the book of Isaiah that pertains to the ancient king of Babylon about 650 years before Christ lived. As we have discussed, prophecy often uses allegorical people and terms. This prophecy has been viewed as an indictment against Satan himself; the true spiritual king of the Babylonian world-system. Taking that interpretation of this account, it serves as an inside look at the reason why Satan was cast out of Heaven, his ravaging of the nations, and his descent into the Abyss (Hell).

Isaiah writes:

> *"The realm of the dead below is all astir to meet*
> *you at your coming; it rouses the spirits of the departed*
> *to greet you—all those who were leaders in the world; it*
> *makes them rise from their thrones—all those who were*
> *kings over the nations. They will all respond, they will*
> *say to you, "**You also have become weak, as we are;***
> ***you have become like us.**" All your pomp has been*
> *brought down to the grave, along with the noise of your*
> *harps; maggots are spread out beneath you and worms*
> *cover you. **How you have fallen from heaven, Lucifer***

126

(morning star), son of the dawn. **You have been cast down to the earth,** *you who once laid low the nations!*

You said in your heart, **"I will ascend to the heavens; I will raise my throne** *above the stars of God;* **I will sit enthroned** *on the mount of assembly, on the utmost heights of Mount Zaphon.* **I will ascend above the tops of the clouds; I will make myself like the Most High.** *" But you are brought down to the realm of the dead, to the depths of the pit. Those who see you stare at you, they ponder your fate: "Is this the man who shook the earth and made kingdoms tremble, the man who made the world a wilderness, who overthrew its cities and* **would not let his captives go home?** *"*

All the kings of the nations lie in state, each in his own tomb. But you are cast out of your tomb like **a rejected branch** *you are covered with the slain, with those pierced by the sword, those who descend to the stones of the pit. Like a corpse trampled underfoot, you will not join them in burial, for you have destroyed your land and killed your people. Let the offspring of the wicked never be mentioned again. Prepare a place to slaughter his children for the sins of their ancestors;* **they are not to rise to inherit the land and cover the earth with their cities.** *"I will rise up against them,"* declares the Lord Almighty. *(Isa.14: 9-22 NIV)*

Such a detailed prophecy can be speaking of none other than Satan's fate on the Day of Judgement. Unfortunately, he will be released from the Abyss for a short time but his final judgement is destined to be the lake of fire along with the Beast and the False Prophet.

Chapter 22

The King Rewards the Faithful

(The Apostles John and Peter hurry to the tomb on the morning of the Resurrection 1898)
Eugene Burnand

After King Jesus has put down all of His enemies **the Kingdom of God will be established at last**! Jesus Christ will restore order to the earth once and for all by instituting the government of Heaven. He will not do this wonderful work of restoration alone but the saints who were faithful to Him during their lifetimes will be there to assist Him in the Kingdom.

The first order of business is that the King will give the saints new resurrected bodies. This phenomenon will occur as soon as the saints in Heaven return with Jesus and those alive see Him. John notes that 'once we see Jesus we will become exactly like Him because we will finally see Him as He truly is'.(1 John 3:2) Since no man can see God and live Paul informs us that this is also the exact moment that our bodies will be changed to become like His body.

By studying Jesus' body after His resurrection we can gather many clues as to what these new bodies will be like. They will look like a blend between our normal bodies now and the celestial bodies of angels. They will have a heavenly glow about them. We will still have the ability to eat, drink and converse but these bodies will have extraordinary qualities as well. We will be able to move through matter as Jesus did after He rose from the dead. We will be able to travel through space-time by disappearing from one place and manifesting in another. We also will have the ability to ascend into heaven and back down to earth as the angels do. This is exactly what Christ Himself did upon His ascension. These glorious bodies will not be contaminated with sin, sickness or disease of any kind. They will be strong and beautiful bodies that never wear out with age or fatigue.

Each of the saints will manifest as the true "Sons of God". Every single one of us will be completely filled with the Spirit, knowledge, power and love of God at all times. What's more is that each of our bodies will be perfectly crafted expressions that fit our uniqueness! If we just think of how beautiful and unique every expression of creation is now our imagination may be able to scratch the surface of what God has planned for those who love Him. Our current bodies are in "seed form" now but once we are translated they will be in "bloom." Consider how different a flower is from a seed and this may help illustrate the contrast.

Paul wrote extensively about this to the Corinthian church:

"*So also is **the resurrection of the dead**. It is sown in corruption; it is raised in incorruption: It is sown in dishonour; it is raised in glory: it is sown in weakness; it is raised in power: It is sown a natural body; it is raised a spiritual body. There is a natural body, and there is a spiritual body. And so it is written, **The first man Adam was made a living soul; the last Adam was made a quickening spirit**. Howbeit that was not first which is spiritual, but that which is natural; and afterward that which is spiritual. The first man is of the earth, earthy; the second man is the Lord from heaven. As is the earthy, such are they also that are earthy: and as is the heavenly, such are they also that are heavenly. **And as we have borne the image of the earthy, we shall also bear the image of the heavenly**. Now this I say, brethren, that flesh and blood cannot inherit the kingdom of God; neither doth corruption inherit incorruption. Behold, I shew you a mystery; We shall not all sleep, but **we shall all be changed**, In a moment, in the twinkling of an eye, at the last trump: for the trumpet shall sound, and **the dead shall be raised incorruptible**,* *and we shall be changed. For this corruptible must put on incorruption, and **this mortal must put on immortality.** "(1 Cor. 15:42-53 NIV)*

The resurrected bodies are essential because in the beginning **God gave dominion over earth to men not to disembodied spirits.** God always keeps His word and so the new bodies give the spirits of the saints the legal right to rule on earth with the resurrected King. The earth has been waiting since the days of Adam for the true "Sons of God" to be revealed. Those who would do the good works that God the Father has prepared for them since before the world began. During Jesus' reign this will finally occur. **The righteous will literally shine like stars in the Kingdom of God as the Lord promised.**

The reason that the Lord is going to have the saints with Him in His Kingdom is for one purpose; **to reign!** We as believers will finally actualize the purpose for which we have been created. We will not be awarded this is honor because the Lord needs help nor is this a position that anyone deserves. The Lord gives offices of rulership to His family members simply because He loves us.

John wrote:

*"And I saw thrones, and they sat upon them, and judgment was given unto them: and I saw the souls of them that were beheaded for the witness of Jesus, and for the word of God, and which had not worshipped the Beast, neither his image, neither had received his mark upon their foreheads, or in their hands; and **they lived and reigned with Christ a thousand years**....Blessed and holy is he that hath part in the first resurrection"*
(Rev. 20:4,6 NIV)

131

This is what Jesus was speaking about all along.

He taught, Blessed be ye poor **(now)**: for yours is the kingdom of God **(then)**.

Blessed are ye that hunger **now**: for ye shall be filled **(then)**.

Blessed are ye that weep **now**: for ye shall laugh **(then)**.

Blessed are ye, when men shall hate you, and when they shall separate you from their company, and shall reproach you, and cast out your name as evil, for the Son of man's sake **(now)**.

Rejoice ye in that day, and leap for joy: for, behold, your reward is great in Heaven

(In the Kingdom of Heaven then)

(Luke 6: 20-23 NIV)

The King promised that if His faithful servants would trust Him and follow Him during His hour of disgrace He would not forget them when He came into His Kingdom. Just as David's men were faithful to him when he was not recognized by Israel as their king so the saints have been faithful to Jesus even though He was not recognized by this world as King. Equally so, when David was finally enthroned His faithful men were given positions of power as well.

Luke recorded this statement Jesus made:

> *"He said therefore, A certain Nobleman went into a far country to receive for Himself a Kingdom, and to return...And it came to pass, that **when He had returned**, having received the Kingdom, then He commanded these servants to be called unto Him, to whom He had given the money, that He might know how much every man had gained by trading. Then came the first, saying, Lord, thy pound hath gained ten pounds. And He said unto him, **Well, thou good servant: because thou hast been faithful in a very little, have thou authority over ten cities**..."*

(Luke 19: 12-17 NIV)

In this parable Jesus explained that those of His disciple who were faithful to Him with their gifts in this world-system will be handsomely rewarded in the visible Kingdom of God. Moreover the servant's reward in the Kingdom is directly proportionate to his service in this world. The Lord has endowed Kingdom citizens with: the full counsel of Scripture, the gift of Salvation, the Holy Spirit, spiritual gifts, leaders in the Body of Christ and a world-wide family. He expects a return on His investments. A strong word of warning is due here. If we study the end of Jesus' parable we clearly see that not only did the unprofitable servant **NOT** inherit the Kingdom of God but his fate was much worse. Many theologians try to re-interpret this to apply to a certain people group but I caution the reader to be very careful. If we are inclined to respect the words of an earthly king as law how much more the King of kings?

It should be noted that not everyone will be destroyed on the Day of the Lord. Some people will be left from every nation to repopulate the earth. This truth makes for very interesting circumstances on planet Earth at that time. During the millennial reign there will be two visible species of man! The two groups will be the old sons of Adam and the new Sons of God. The truth is that there are two species of men on earth now the latter simply has yet to be revealed. The sons of Adam will be blessed, protected, guided and educated by the Sons of God. Just as the Devil now has principalities and powers in heavenly places, once they are cast out the Sons of God will be the new princes over cities and countries.

The old "Sons of God" who fell into sin will be displaced and the new Sons of God who have been redeemed from sin will be installed. The new Sons of God will assist in judging both men and angels! (1 Cor. 6:3) The Lord Himself even promised the disciples that they would sit with Him enthroned in His Kingdom judging the twelve tribes of Israel. That said, the reader should be sure to help the city where they live as much as they can now; who knows, you may be set to judge there in the Kingdom of God.

God was not being allegorical when He said 'the meek shall inherit the earth.'

He meant just what He said.

(Psalms 37)

134

Chapter 23

The King Heals the Earth

(The Garden of Eden 1829)
Thomas Cole

The Lord will heal the land. This will be a time of great refreshing for the earth as it has long awaited for the proper nurturing for which it was created. In that day we will finally see what the earth can do!

Zechariah prophesied:

"The seed will grow well, the vine will yield its fruit, the ground will produce its crops, and the heavens will drop their dew." (Zech. 8:12 NIV)

The Lord will make the entire earth look like Eden. This was exactly the charge that God the Father gave Adam in the beginning but he failed to do so. Jesus, on the other hand, will succeed. He will serve as both the Governor and Officiant who oversees this most sacred work. There will be no spots, wrinkles or blemishes on the earth as the King is known to "thoroughly purge His winnowing floor."

A fascinating series of facts about Jesus being the ultimate caretaker of the earth in the Kingdom of God are:

- *Adam was given the charge to manage the ground*
- *The cursed earth bore thorns and thistles*
- *Jesus as the "Seed" of Abraham was promised land*
- *He is called a Branch and a Fruitful Vine*
- *When He died He wore a crown of thorns (Symbolizing the victory over cursed earth)*
- *The dying thief asked to enter the Kingdom and Jesus promised him Paradise (another name for Eden)*

- *When Jesus rose again He was mistaken for the gardener*
- *He is called the last Adam*
- *He was sown as a Seed and has reaped a harvest of souls*

King Jesus will get the earth ready to be offered back up to the Father. God created this earth as a gift for His Holy Son Jesus and the Son will present it back to the Father in the condition of perfection that He always intended it to be in. This explains why God is not just going to annihilate the earth. He loves the earth. The Father is still patiently working all things towards their expected end. At last, Jesus will make sure that the Father has His heart's desire; a beautiful, clean, orderly, and robust earth that is carefully managed by His faithful children. The King will personally ensure that the Father's Kingdom has come and His will has been done here on Earth exactly as it is in Heaven.

The Lord will heal the animals. Even the animals will be at peace with each other. I can put forth a few thoughts which may assist in the comprehensibility of this truth. First, In the garden of Eden all animals were vegetarian. This is not hard to believe. If a giant elephant can be sustained on plant life can't something as small as a cheetah? There also may have been a much greater variety of vegetation than we could possibly imagine in our current age. These plants could suit the dietary needs of our most ravenous hunters without a problem. After all, God made them; He knows exactly what they need. Second, the animals did not attack each other on Noah's ark. In fact, God directed them right to Noah. No doubt carnivorous animals walked right past their prey without issue. Animals who are mortal

137

enemies abode together peacefully for 40 days without a problem.

Isaiah prophesied the following about Jesus' Kingdom:

"The wolf will live with the lamb, the leopard will lie down with the goat, the calf and the lion and the yearling together; and a little child will lead them. The cow will feed with the bear, their young will lie down together, and the lion will eat straw like the ox. The infant will play near the cobra's den, and the young child will put its hand into the viper's nest. They will neither harm nor destroy on all My holy mountain, **for the earth will be filled with the knowledge of the Lord as the waters cover the sea.***"*

(Isa.11:6-9 NIV)

God is going to fill all living things with a great knowledge of who He is and what He desires. The result will be what occurred between Daniel and the lions in that terrifying den. Both man and beast were filled with the knowledge of God's will and neither did the other any harm.

The Lord will heal the sons of Adam. While, this branch of men will still struggle with sin until the time of the New Heavens and New Earth they will be much better off in Christ's Kingdom than they are now. The sons of Adam will go back to being healthy and vibrant. Men and women will be as strong and old as the people in the book of Genesis. Looking back we find that the oldest man who ever lived was Methuselah and he lived to be 969 years old!

Isaiah saw the future days of Jerusalem in the Kingdom and reported:

> *"Never again will there be in it an infant who lives but a few days or an old man who does not live out his years; the one who dies at a hundred will be thought a mere child; the one who fails to reach a hundred will be considered accursed. They will build houses and dwell in them; they will plant vineyards and eat their fruit. No longer will they build houses and others live in them, or plant and others eat. For* **as the days of a tree, so will be the days of My people***; My chosen ones will long enjoy the work of their hands. They will not labour in vain, nor will they bear children doomed to misfortune; for they will be a people blessed by the Lord, they and their descendants with them. Before they call I will answer; while they are still speaking I will hear. I will rejoice over Jerusalem and take delight in My people; the sound of weeping and of crying will be heard in it no more."* (Isa. 65:20-24 NIV)

At such an abundant time I hardly suspect that men will fear death as they do now. The Lord will be visible shining like the sun and the saints will be as the stars of heaven. After a person has lived a long and full life they will be ready to simply transition into the next phase of life. It is also written that **the study of war will cease.** Since Cain murdered Abel the blood of innocent victims has been crying out to the Lord of hosts for vengeance. In those days of Christ's Kingdom people will no longer be violent towards each other. The study of war will come to an end as the survivors of God's wrath will "beat their swords into plowshares." (Isa. 2:4)The gifts that God gave to men will all be redeemed. People will no longer use their brilliance for the art of war but for the sake of peace

Chapter 24

The King as the Glory of the Nations

(The Holy City)

The Lord will establish Jerusalem as the capital of the new world. People from all of the newly populated nations will flock to Jerusalem to join the restored Jews. Jesus will establish His throne in the city of the Great King. From here the Lord is going to issue the decrees of God. The global laws will truly come from Zion. So, in the Kingdom of God we will have a one world government but it will be a Kingdom that is established in righteousness. There will be no democracy, republic, parliament or voting. The word of King Jesus will be international law.

Each nation will be required to participate in the holy feast of tabernacles otherwise known as Sukkot. This feast was a celebration that Jews were supposed to have in order to thank God for the harvest. It was the only feast that the Jews were allowed to have a Gentile or Goyim partake in. Sukkot foreshadowed the time when King Jesus would open up Israel and welcome all nations in for worship.

It is written:

"In His name shall the gentiles trust…" (Matt. 12:21 NIV) and the Lord promised "My house shall be a house of prayer for all nations." (Matt. 21:13 NIV)

In the Kingdom of Christ the ancestral Hebrews will be an especially blessed people.

Zechariah prophesied:

*"The word of the Lord Almighty came to me. This is what the Lord Almighty says: "I am very jealous for Zion; I am burning with jealousy for her." This is what the Lord says: "**I will return to Zion and dwell in Jerusalem.** Then Jerusalem will be called the Faithful*

City, and the mountain of the Lord Almighty will be called the Holy Mountain." This is what the Lord Almighty says: "Once again men and women of ripe old age will sit in the streets of Jerusalem, each of them with cane in hand because of their age. The city streets will be filled with boys and girls playing there." This is what the Lord Almighty says: "It may seem marvellous to the remnant of this people at that time, but will it seem marvellous to Me?" declares the Lord Almighty. This is what the Lord Almighty says: **"I will save my people** from the countries of the east and the west. **I will bring them back to live in Jerusalem**; they will be My people, and I will be faithful and righteous to them as their God."

This is what the Lord Almighty says: "Just as I had determined to bring disaster on you and showed no pity when your ancestors angered Me," says the Lord Almighty, "so now I have determined to do good again to Jerusalem and Judah. Do not be afraid. These are the things you are to do: Speak the truth to each other, and render true and sound judgment in your courts; do not plot evil against each other, and do not love to swear falsely. I hate all this," declares the Lord.

This is what the Lord Almighty says: "The fasts of the fourth, fifth, seventh and tenth months will become joyful and glad occasions and happy festivals for Judah. Therefore love truth and peace." This is what the Lord Almighty says: **"Many peoples and the inhabitants of many cities will yet come**, and the inhabitants of one city will go to another and say, '**Let us go at once to entreat the Lord** and seek the Lord Almighty. I myself am going.' And **many peoples and powerful nations will come to Jerusalem to seek the Lord Almighty and to entreat Him**." This is what the Lord Almighty says: "In *those days ten people from all languages and nations will take firm hold of one Jew by the hem of his robe and say, 'Let us go with you, because we have heard that God is with you.'* (Zech. 8:1-8, 14-17, 19-23□ NIV)

God will restore and bless the Jews in a way they have never been blessed before. The Father is jealous for the true Zion and once the veil is lifted from their eyes this most zealous nation will finally see what was before them all along. ***Rebbe Melech HaMoshiach Yehoshua*** is indeed the promised descendant of David and King of Israel. He is not just King of Israel but King of the entire Earth. Once this is clear then truly all Israel (both the natural and spiritual Jews) will be saved. This great nation will finally be redeemed and safe as God promised it would. All of the nations around it will be at peace with it and boatloads of resources will flow into it from around the world as an offering to the King of kings. No one will need to buy or sell there because of its abundance. The visitors will not be treated as outcasts but beloved younger brothers. The blessed Jewish elders will never again shut up the Kingdom of God but gladly teach the world the ways of the God of Israel.

In the end, Jesus the King of kings will present a perfected earth and humanity to the Father and then God will be all in all through the presence of the Holy Spirit. It will be as when King David had given so much wealth to build the temple and the leaders inspired by his example did the same. The people willing gave as well because David had proven to be a man after God's own heart.

King David praised the Lord in the presence of the whole assembly, saying,

"Praise be to You, Lord,

the God of our father Israel,

from everlasting to everlasting.

Yours, Lord, is the greatness and the power

and the glory and the majesty and the splendor,

for everything in Heaven and Earth is Yours.

Yours, Lord, is the Kingdom;

You are exalted as Head over all.

Wealth and honor come from You;

You are the Ruler of all things.

In Your hands are strength and power

to exalt and give strength to all.

Now, our God, we give you thanks,

and praise Your glorious Name…"

(1 Chro. 29:10-13 NIV)

So be it on earth as it is in Heaven. May Your Kingdom come Father. This we pray in the name of Jesus Christ, the King of kings and Lord of lords.

Amen.

Afterword:

I pray that you have been edified and encouraged by this work. By tracing the theme of the Kingdom of God through the scriptures we have clearly identified the unifying theme between the Old and New testaments. For those who are already citizens in the Kingdom of God I encourage you to be filled with the Holy Spirit daily. Go and make disciples of Christ everywhere by baptizing them in the name of Jesus for the forgiveness of sins and teach them to obey all that King Jesus taught. Pray for the sick, cast out demons and be led by the Holy Spirit in all you do. Remember that the Kingdom of God is not only in words but in power. Live every day in the presence of the Lord and whatever you do, do it unto His glory. On your job, in your home and in your community serve the King in word and deed. We are still in this world- system but we are not of it. Our citizenship is in Heaven and we are called to walk everyday as ambassadors of Christ.

To those who **WANT** to enter the Kingdom of God follow these simple steps:

- *Repent:* of all of your sins and flee from the coming wrath of God
- *Believe:* In Jesus Christ as the sacrifice for your sin and your Lord
- *Be Baptized*: In Jesus' name into the body of Christ
- *Receive the Holy Spirit:* the Kingdom power from Heaven
- *Abide:* in Christ by reading and obeying the Bible

146

- ***Confide:*** in faithful brothers or sisters in a good local meeting of believers
- ***Multiply:*** be fruitful by sharing the Gospel of the Kingdom
- ***Grow in Grace:*** when you fall into sin don't wallow, repent and get back in line
- ***Finish the Race:*** remain faithful, fruitful, Spirit-filled and obedient until the end.

References:

Artwork Citations:

Argenton, Rodrigo Tesuto. "Yellow Jesus Cropped and Edited." 26 Oct.
2013. *Wikimedia Commons*, (Used as Cover Art)
    Wikimedia, 30 June. 2015, commons.wikimedia.org/wiki/
    File: https://commons.wikimedia.org/wiki/File:Yellow_Jesus_-
_Edited_and_croped.jpg. Accessed 18 May. 2017.

Baker, Thomas. *Ufton Church*. 1 Jan. 1861. *Wikimedia Commons*,
Wikimedia, 4 Feb.
    2012,
commons.wikimedia.org/wiki/File:Baker_UftonChurch_HAGAM.jpg.
Accessed
    21 Apr. 2017.

Buonarroti, Michelangelo. *The Creation of Adam*. 1 Jan. 1511. *Wikimedia
Commons*,
    Wikimedia, 9 June 2011, commons.wikimedia.org/wiki/Adam#/media/
    File:Creaci%C3%B3n_de_Ad%C3%A1n_(Miguel_%C3%81ngel).jpg
. Accessed 14 Apr.
    2017.

Burnand, Eugene. *The Apostles John and Peter hurry to the tomb on the
morning of*
    the Resurrection. 1 Jan. 1898. *Wikimedia Commons*, Wikimedia, 17 Apr.
2017,
    commons.wikimedia.org/wiki/File:Disciples_running_by_EB.jpg.
Accessed 22
    Apr. 2017.

Caravaggio, Michelangelo Merisi da. "The Martyrdom of St. Matthew."
1 Jan. 1599.
    Wikimedia Commons, Wikimedia, 9 June 2011,
commons.wikimedia.org/wiki/
    File:Michelangelo_Merisi_da_Caravaggio_-
_The_Martyrdom_of_St_Matthew_-_WGA04121.j
    pg. Accessed 21 Apr. 2017.

148

Cleve III, Hendrick Van. *The Tower of Babel*. 1 Jan. 1500. *Wikimedia Commons*,
    Wikimedia, 14 Nov. 2015, commons.wikimedia.org/wiki/
    File:Cleve-van_construction-tower-babel.jpg. Accessed 22 Apr. 2017.

Cole, Thomas. *The Garden of Eden*. 1 Jan. 1829. *Wikimedia Commons*,
Wikimedia, 11
    June 2009, commons.wikimedia.org/wiki/
    File:Cole_Thomas_The_Garden_of_Eden_1828.jpg. Accessed 22 Apr.
2017.

Cooper, Colin Campbell. "The Rush Hour; New York City." 1 Jan. 1900.
    Wikimedia Commons, Wikimedia, 7 Oct. 2012,
commons.wikimedia.org/wiki/
    File:Cooper_Rush_Hour.jpg. Accessed 21 Apr. 2017.

Delacroix, Ferdinand Eugène-Victor. *Sketch for Peace Descends to Earth*.
1 Jan.
    1852. *Wikimedia Commons*, Wikimedia, 9 June 2011,
commons.wikimedia.org/wiki/
    File:Eug%C3%A8ne_Delacroix_-
_Sketch_for_Peace_Descends_to_Earth_-_WGA06217.jpg.
    Accessed 3 Mar. 2016.

Dore, Gusatve. *Illustration for John Milton's Paradise Lost*. 1 Jan. 1866.
    Wikimedia Commons, Wikimedia, 1 Jan. 1866,
commons.wikimedia.org/wiki/
    File:Paradise_Lost_13.jpg. Accessed 14 Apr. 2017.

Dyke, Athony Van. "The Day of Pentecost." 1 Jan. 1618. *Wikimedia Commons*,
    Wikimedia, 24 Jan. 2007, commons.wikimedia.org/wiki/
    File:Anthonis_van_Dyck_-
_Die_Ausgie%C3%9Fung_des_Heiligen_Geistes.jpg.
    Accessed 17 Apr. 2017.

Foster, William A. "The Bible Panorama." 1 Jan. 1891. *Flickr Images*,
Yahoo, 1

Jan. 1891,
www.flickr.com/photos/internetarchivebookimages/14781813691/in/
    photolist-owdEdK-oeZSNJ-owuV2e-of1hNh-owi7eY-of2ah2-of178S-
oyfPmF-owhW3q-of15J9-o
    usH3G-owuXDP-owi2vE-owdvW4-owt4iW-of1zkB-owhw43-owsZRW-
owe29T-oeZRDa-of12gr-of1gq-oeZFL5-of1fqU-owuxh2-of27Tz-owi7PA-
of13Gw-owsVPY-owhPkN-out46C-owt6Md-oeZuLj-ow
    hjP9-owsZAf-oyfnYB-oyff2e-owsVqm-of1sjb-owdCkX-owi7uh-
owv5Uv-oyfjPk-oeZLDG-of1rPp
    -of1qkc-owhvF9-owdeBk-owttdu-oeZvVy. Accessed 16 Apr. 2017.

Greco, El. "Christ Carrying the Cross." 1 Jan. 1590. *Wikimedia
Commons*,
    Wikimedia, 6 Oct. 2012, commons.wikimedia.org/wiki/
    File:El_Greco_-_Christ_Carrying_the_Cross_-
_Google_Art_Project.jpg.
    Accessed 17 Apr. 2017.

Martin, John. *The Great Day of His Wrath*. 1 Jan. 1853. *Wikimedia
Commons*,
    Wikimedia, 14 May 2014, commons.wikimedia.org/wiki/
    File:MARTIN_John_Great_Day_of_His_Wrath.jpg. Accessed 22 Apr.
2017.

Matejko, Jan. "Zboja Stefana Batorego." 1 Jan. 1872. *Wikimedia
Commons*,
    Wikimedia, 7 Feb. 2007, commons.wikimedia.org/wiki/
    File:Zbroja_Stefana_Batorego_Jan_Matejko.PNG. Accessed 21 Apr.
2017.

Millias, John Everette. "Victory O Lord." 1 Jan. 1871. *Wikimedia
Commons*,
    Wikimedia, 17 Jan. 2010, commons.wikimedia.org/wiki/
    File:Millais_Victory_O_Lord.jpg. Accessed 15 Apr. 2017.

Olrik, Henrik. *Sermon on the Mount*. 27 Oct. 2007. *Wikimedia Commons*,
Wikimedia,
    27 Oct. 2007, commons.wikimedia.org/wiki/
    File:Sankt_Matthaeus_Kirke_Copenhagen_altarpiece_detail1.jpg.
    Accessed 21
    Apr. 2017.

Schneider, Sascha. *Mammon and His Slave*. 1 Jan. 1896. *Wikimedia Commons*,
    Wikimedia, 22 Sept. 2013, commons.wikimedia.org/wiki/
    File:Mammon_and_His_Slave.jpg. Accessed 21 Apr. 2017.

Tanner, Henry Ossawa. "Jesus and Nicodemus." 31 Dec. 1989. *Wikimedia Commons*,
    Wikimedia, 21 Feb. 2012, commons.wikimedia.org/wiki/
    File:Henry_Ossawa_Tanner_-_Jesus_and_nicodemus.jpg. Accessed 17
Apr. 2017.

Tissot, James. "The Gathering of Manna." 1 Jan. 1896. *Wikimedia Commons*,
    Wikimedia, 28 Dec. 2009, commons.wikimedia.org/wiki/
    File:Tissot_The_Gathering_of_the_Manna_(color).jpg. Accessed 15
Apr. 2017.

Tissot, James Jacques-Joseph. *The Ark Passes Over the Jordan*. 1 Jan. 1896.
    Wikimedia Commons, Wikimedia, 1 Nov. 2012,
commons.wikimedia.org/wiki/
    File:James_Jacques_Joseph_Tissot_-
_The_Ark_Passes_Over_the_Jordan_-_Google_Art_Pr
    oject.jpg. Accessed 16 Apr. 2017.

Van Oostsanen, Jacob Cornelisz. *The Laughing Fool*. 1 Jan. 1500. *Wikimedia*
    Commons, Wikimedia, 15 Mar. 2016, commons.wikimedia.org/wiki/
    File:Laughing_Fool.jpg. Accessed 22 Apr. 2017.

Vein, Joseph Marie. "Joshuah Ordering the Sun to Stand Still." 1 Jan.
1743.
    Wikimedia Commons, Wikimedia, 1 Sept. 2015,
commons.wikimedia.org/wiki/
    File:Joshuah_Ordering_the_Sun_to_Stand_Still._ca_1743-
1744._Joseph_Marie_Vien.jpg
    . Accessed 16 Apr. 2017.

Literary Citations:

Martyr, Justin. "The Second Apology of Justin Martyr to the Roman
Senate."
  Newadvent.org, Kevin Knight, 1 Jan. 1885,
www.newadvent.org/fathers/
    0127.htm. Accessed 14 Apr. 2017.

Munroe, Dr. Myles. *The Glory of Living*. Shippensburg, PA, Destiny
Image
  Publishing, 2005.

Web Based Citations:

Pawson, David. "The Kingdom." *DavidPawson.org*, 1 Jan. 2013,
davidpawson.org/
    resources/series/the-kingdom. Accessed 17 Apr. 2017.

Reeves, Professor John. "Bereshit Rabbati on Shemhazai & Azael." *UNC
Charlotte*,
    University of North Carolina (UNC Charlotte), 1 Jan. 1940,
    clas-pages.uncc.edu/john-reeves/course-materials/
    rels-2104-hebrew-scripturesold-testament/bereshit-rabbati-on-
shemhazai-azael/.
    Accessed 14 Apr. 2017.

"10 Facts about the Emancipation Proclamation." *Civilwar.org*, Civil
War Trust, 1
    Jan. 2014, www.civilwar.org/education/history/emancipation-150/
    10-facts.html?referrer=https://www.google.com/. Accessed 14 Apr.
2017.

Billups Kingdom Resources LLC. ©2017

Made in the USA
Lexington, KY
06 June 2017